Drawing Sculpture

Drawing Sculpture

Carroll Dunham

Soberscove Press

Chicago

Soberscove Press
Chicago, Illinois
soberscove.com

Drawing Sculpture © 2026 Carroll Dunham

All rights reserved. No part of this publication may be reproduced,
stored in retrieval systems, or transmitted in any form or by
any means, electronic, mechanical, photocopying, recording or
otherwise, without the prior permission of the copyright holder.

Library of Congress Control Number: 2025945975

ISBN 978-1-940190-36-5
Design by Rita Skingle
First Printing, 2026
Printed in Lithuania

Distributed by
ARTBOOK | D.A.P.
75 Broad Street, Suite 630
New York, NY 10004
artbook.com

Cover: *Untitled Sculpture Drawing* (5/31/24), 2024. Conté crayon,
watercolor marker, and pencil on paper. 16¾ x 11½ inches

Contents

Drawings
12/2/23–12/30/24

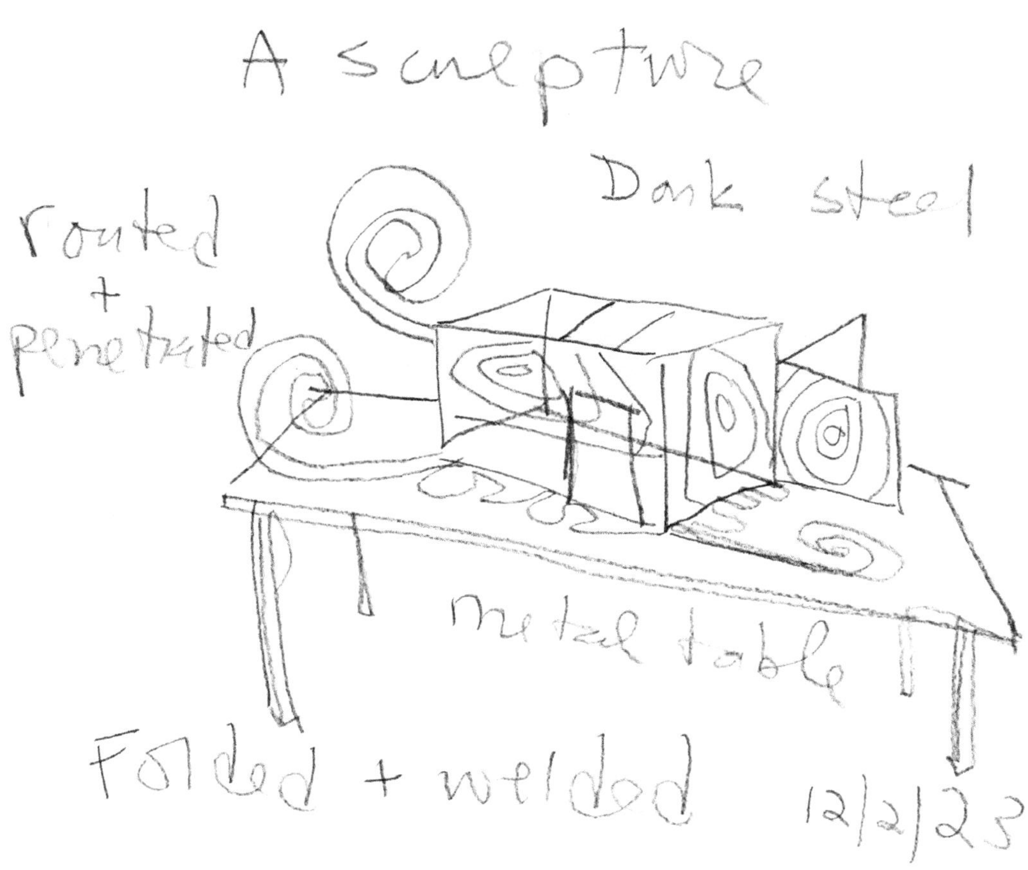
A sculpture
Dark steel
routed
+
penetrated
metal table
Folded + welded   12/2/23

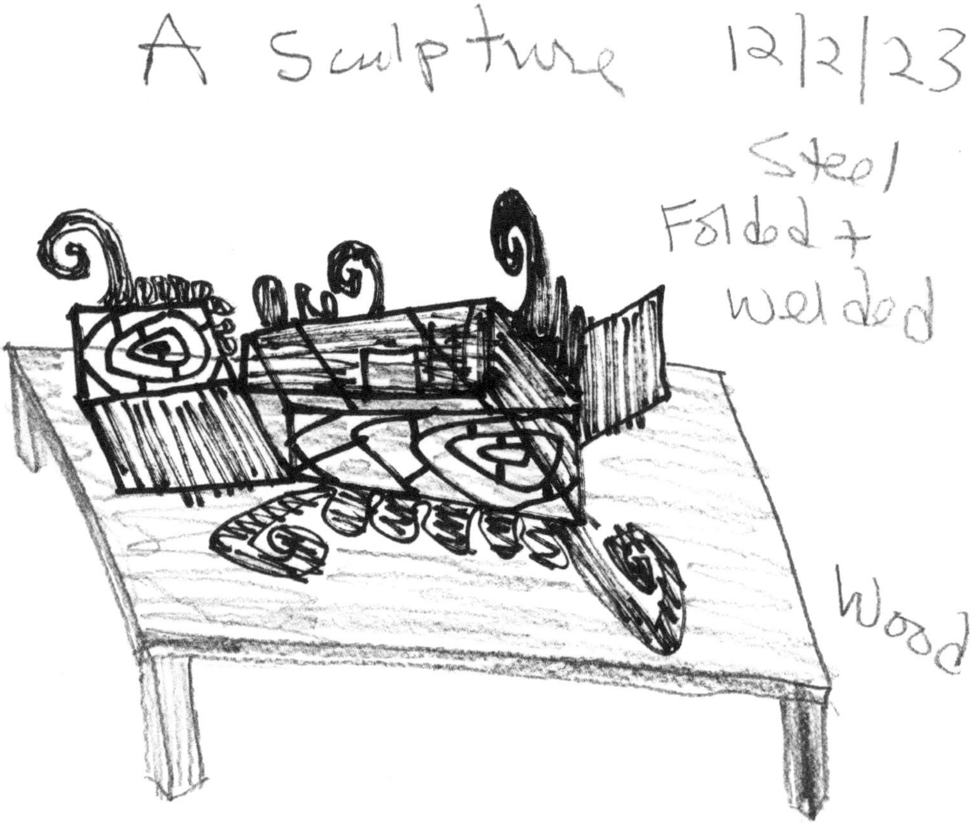

A Sculpture   12/2/23
Steel
Folded +
welded

Wood

12/3/23

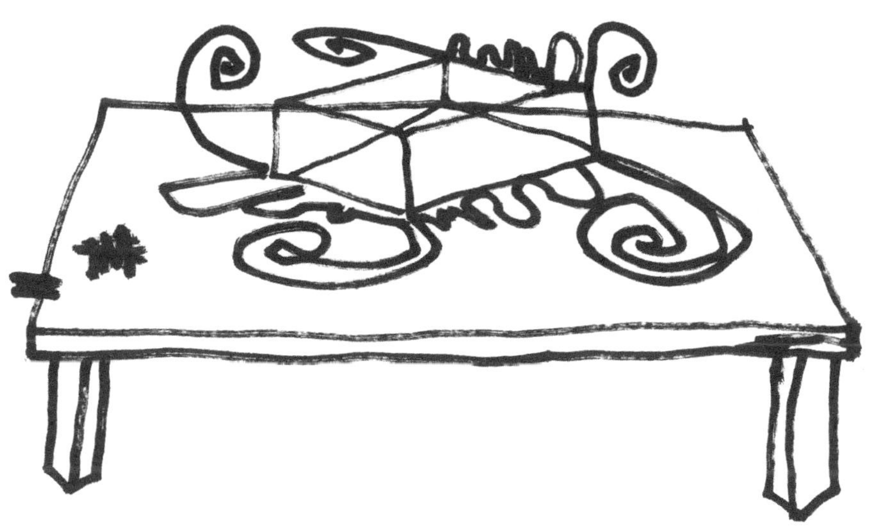

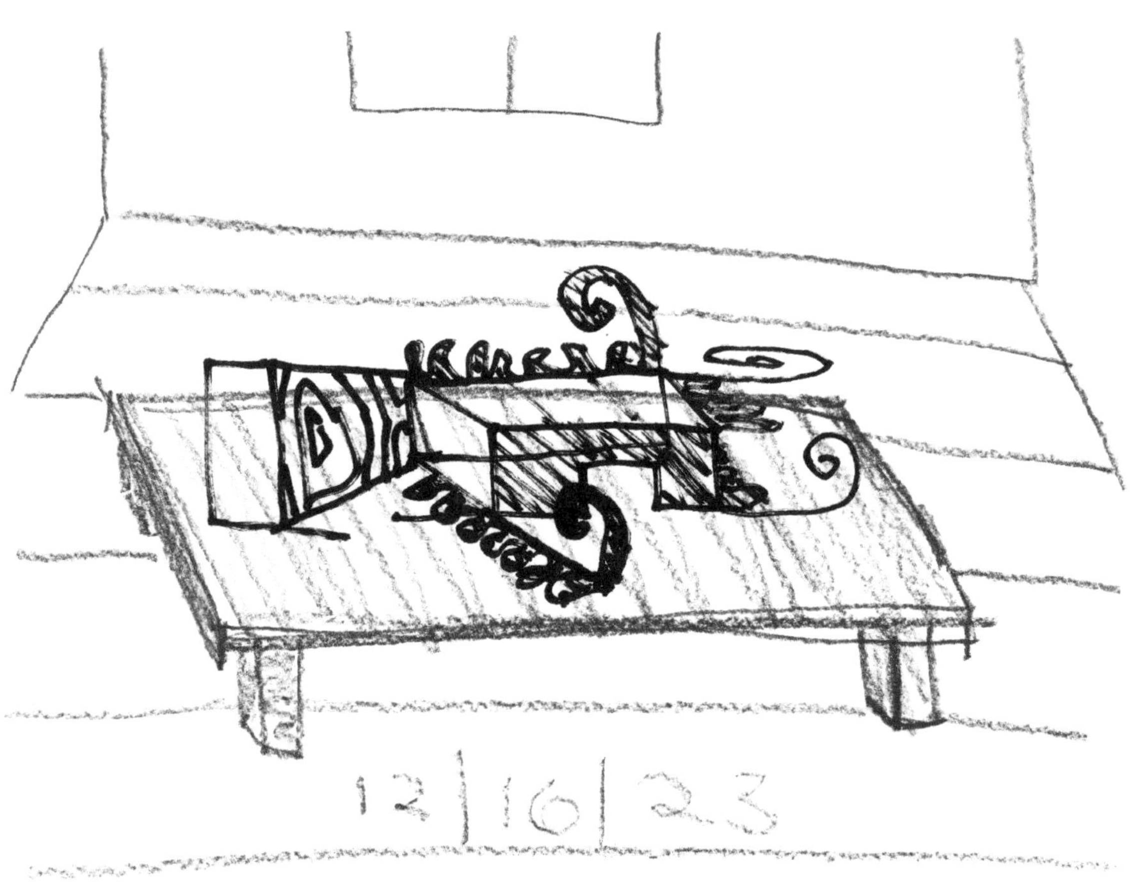

12 | 16 | 23

Dec. 16, 2023

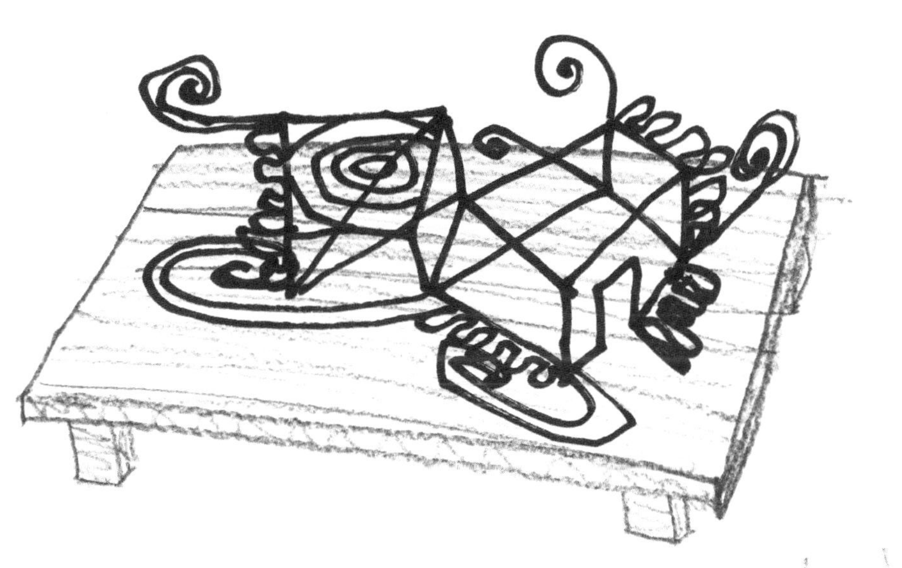

sculpture, wood table

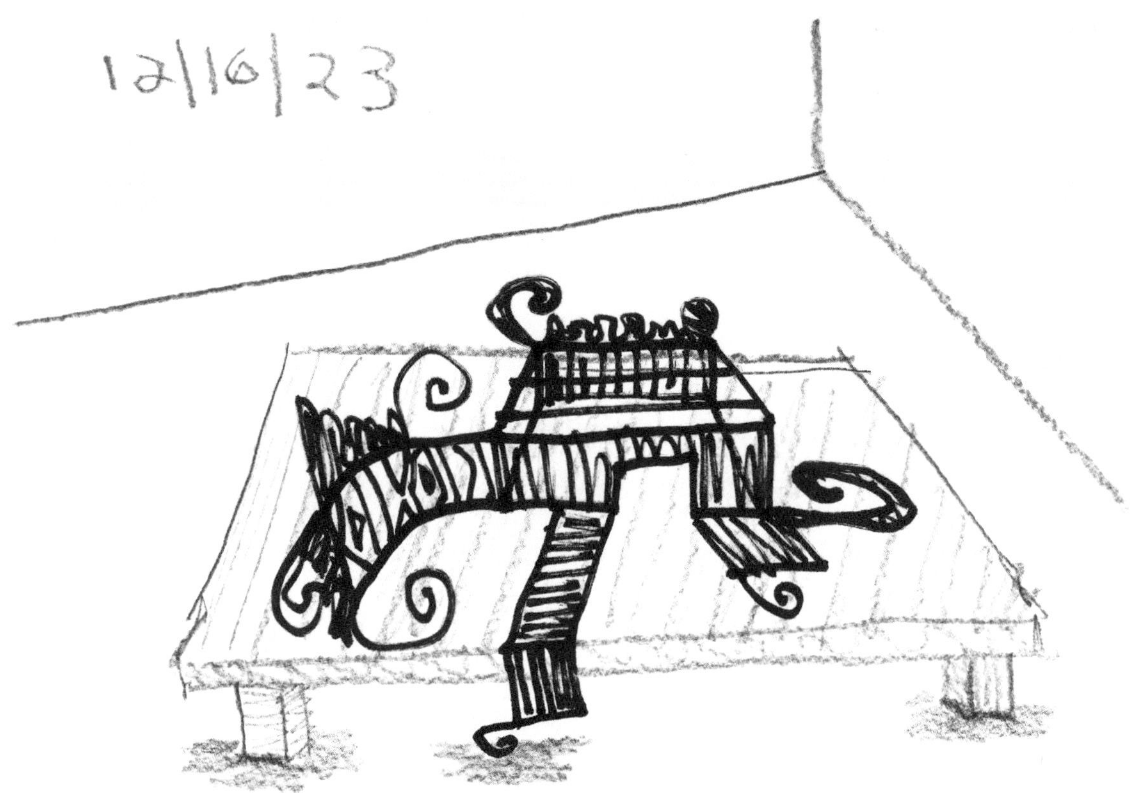

12/16/23

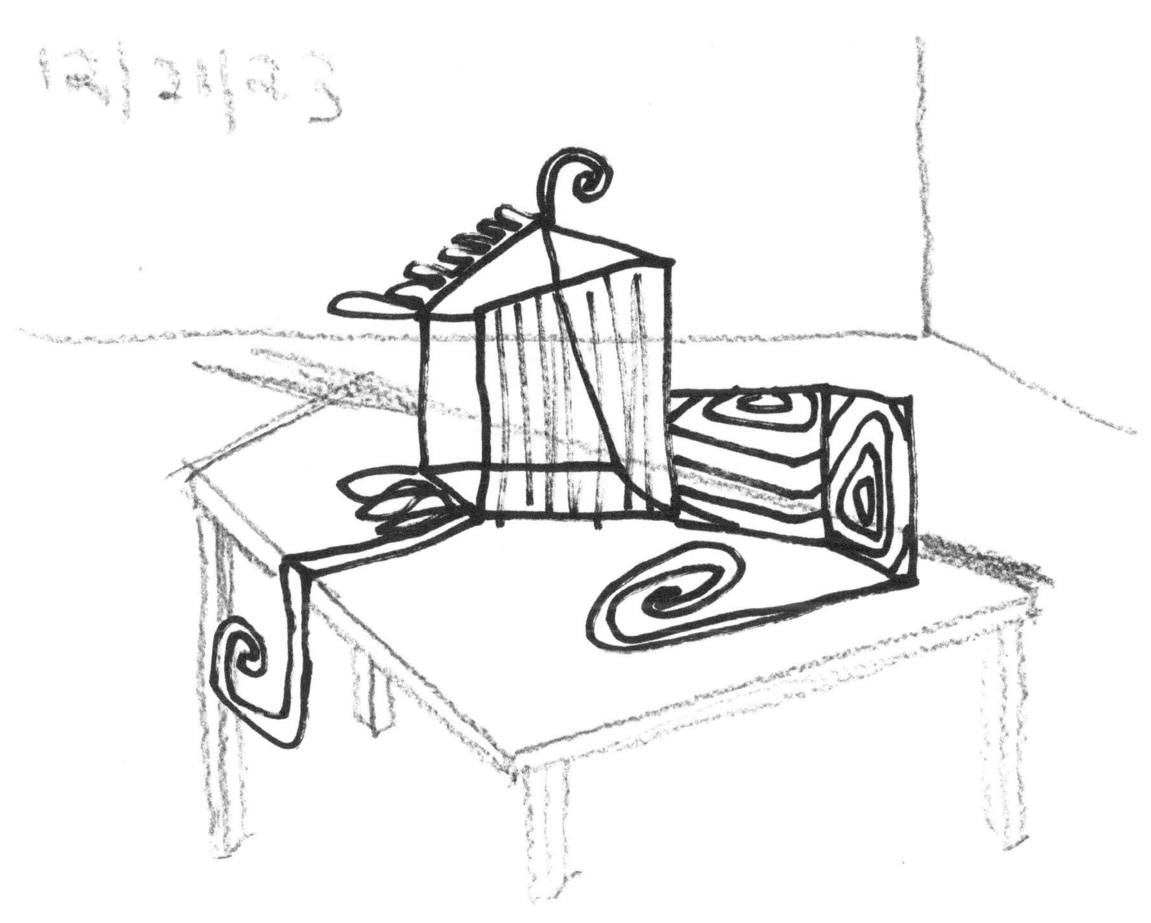

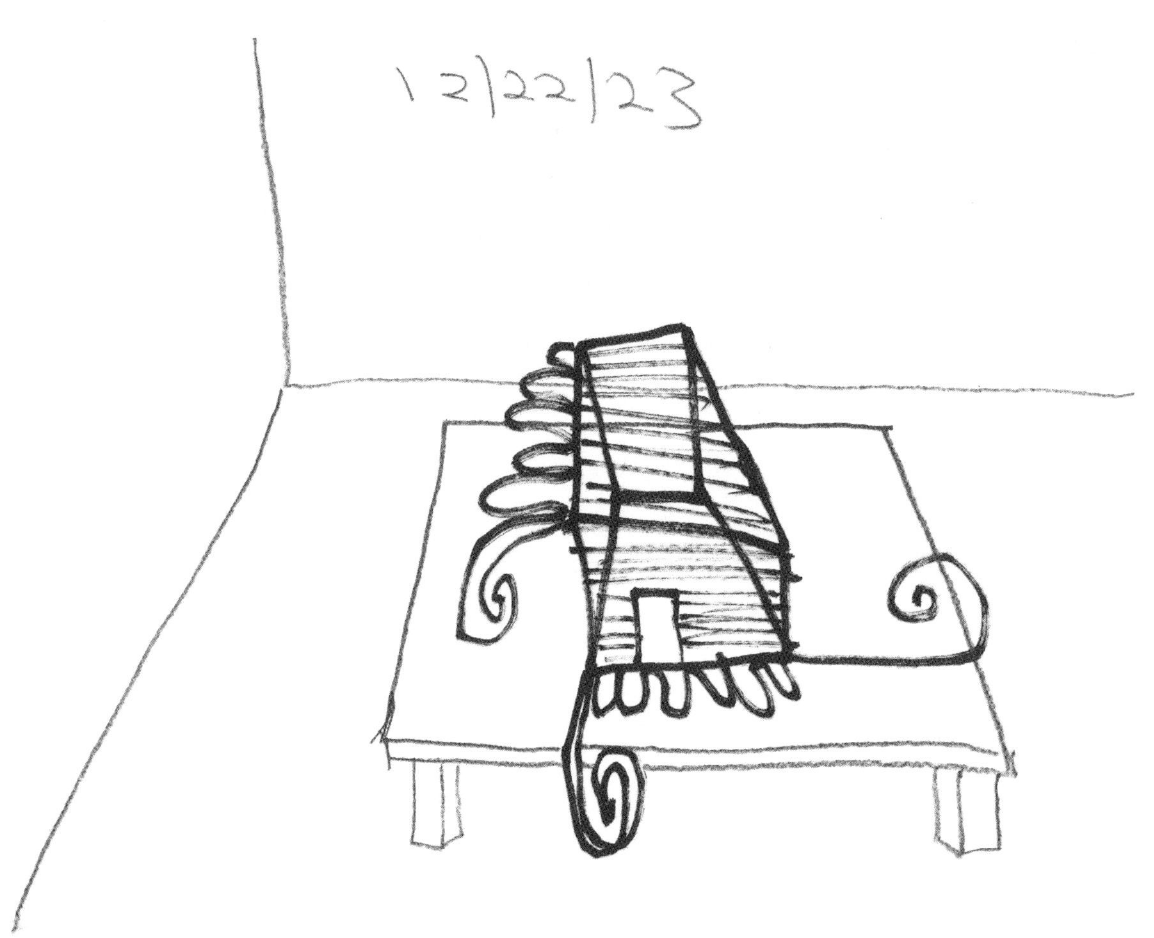

12/22/23

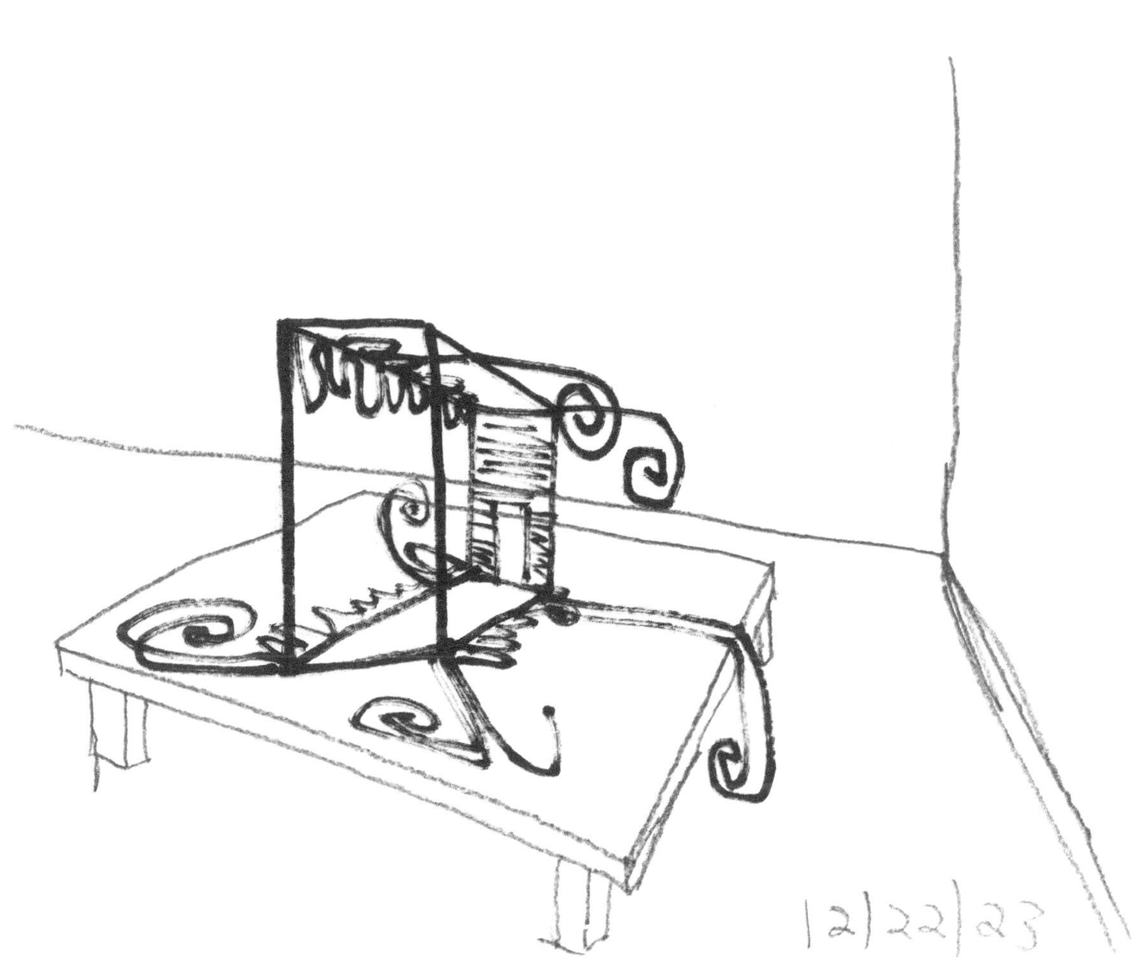

12/22/23

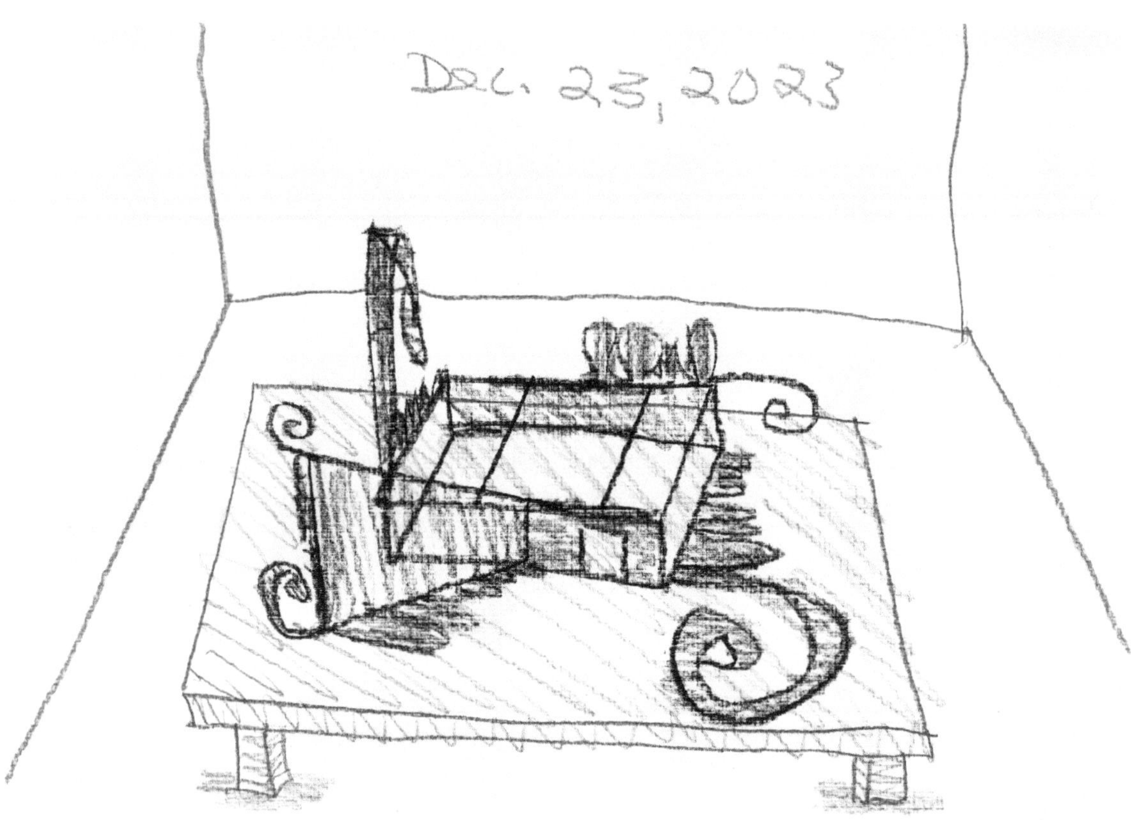
Dec. 23, 2023

Dec. 23, 2023

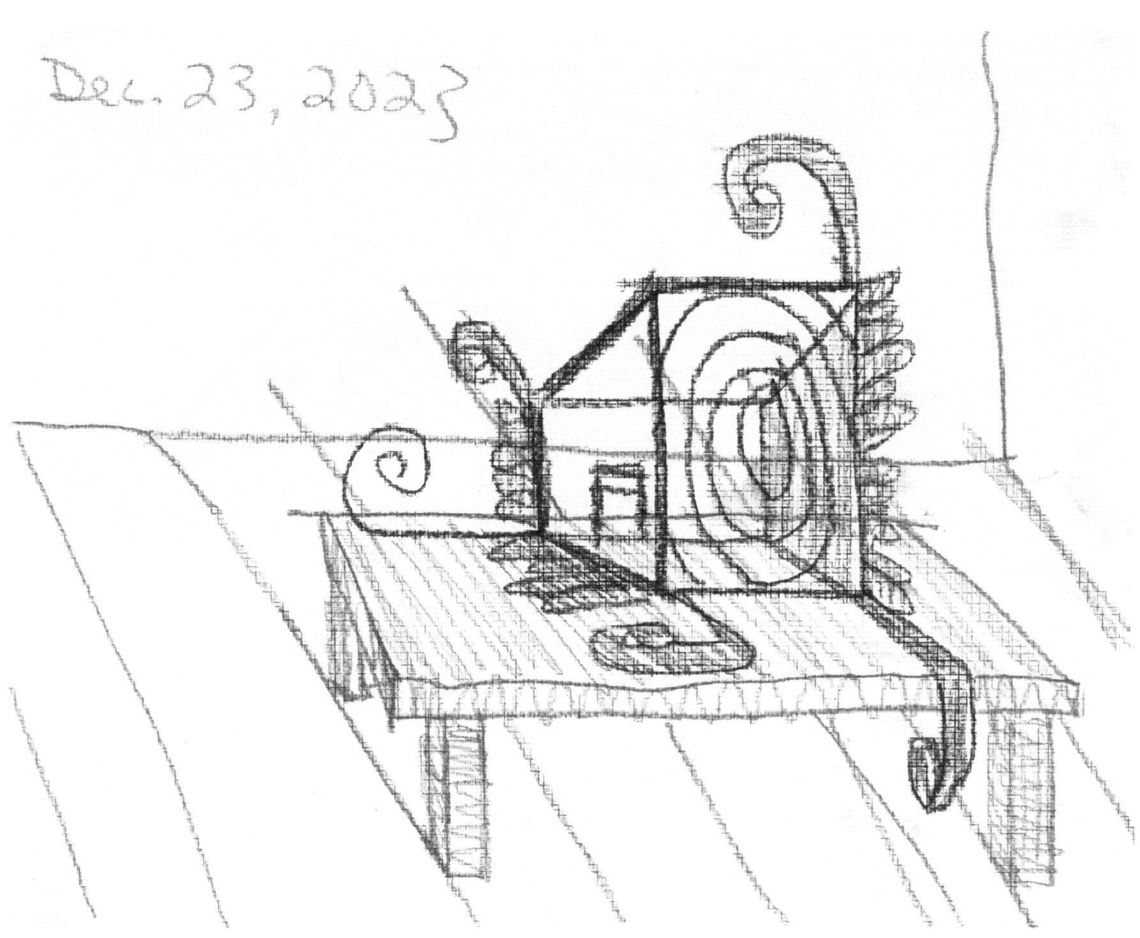

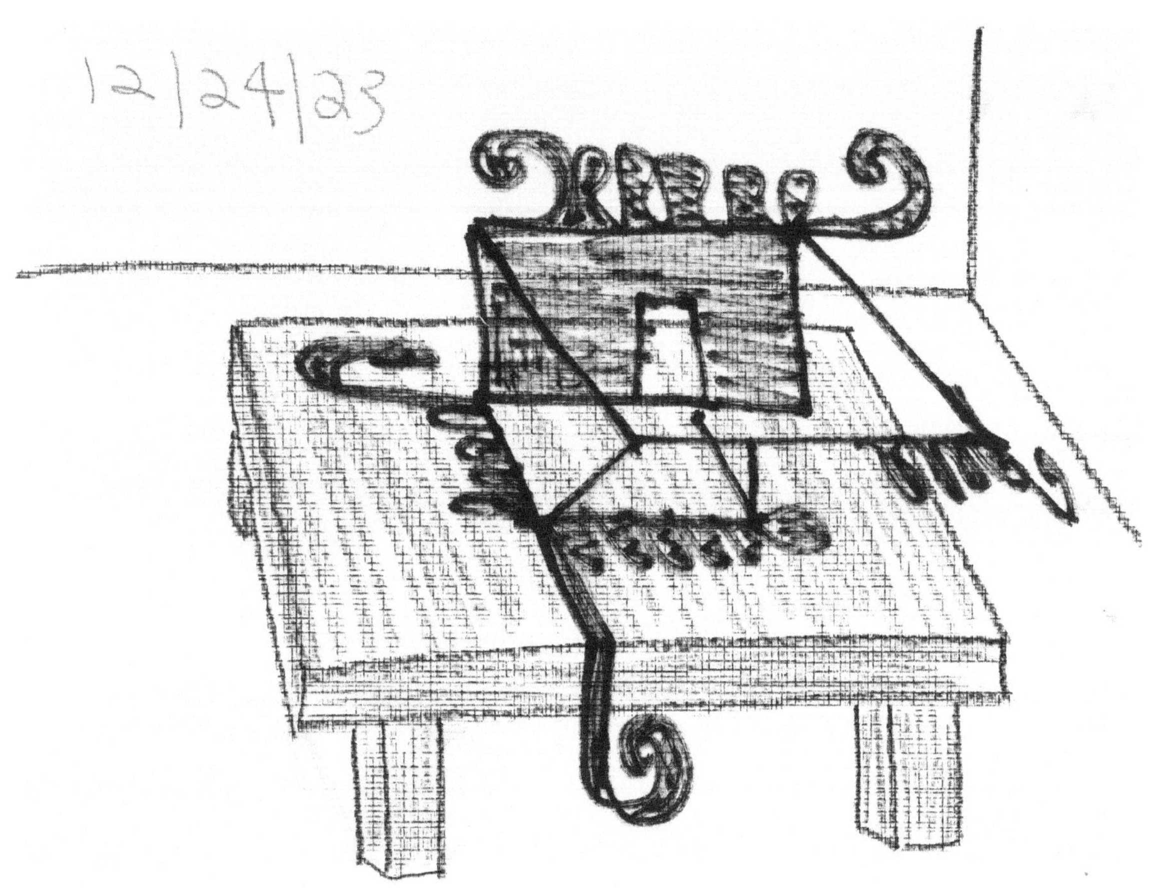

12/24/23

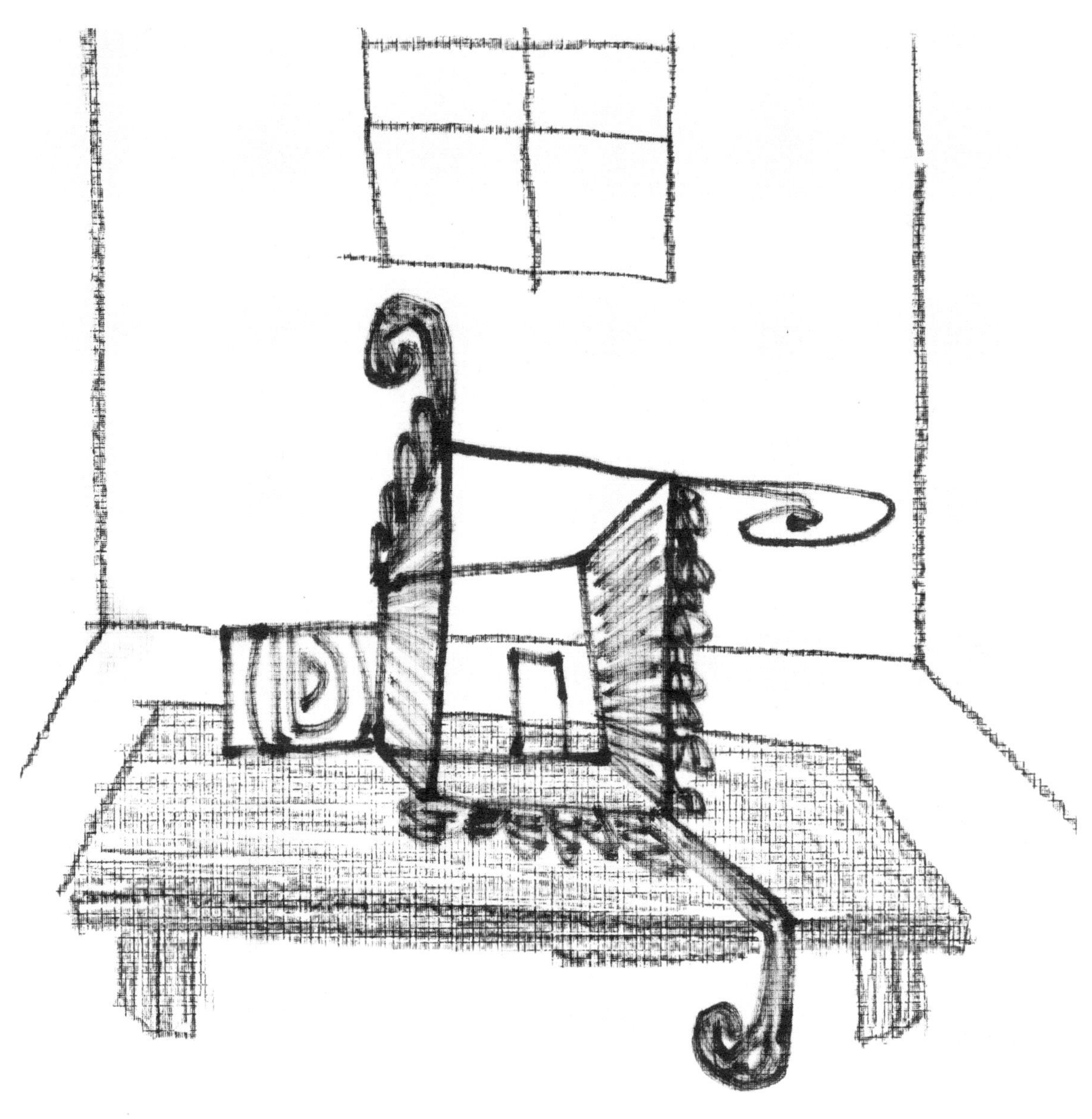

12/26/23

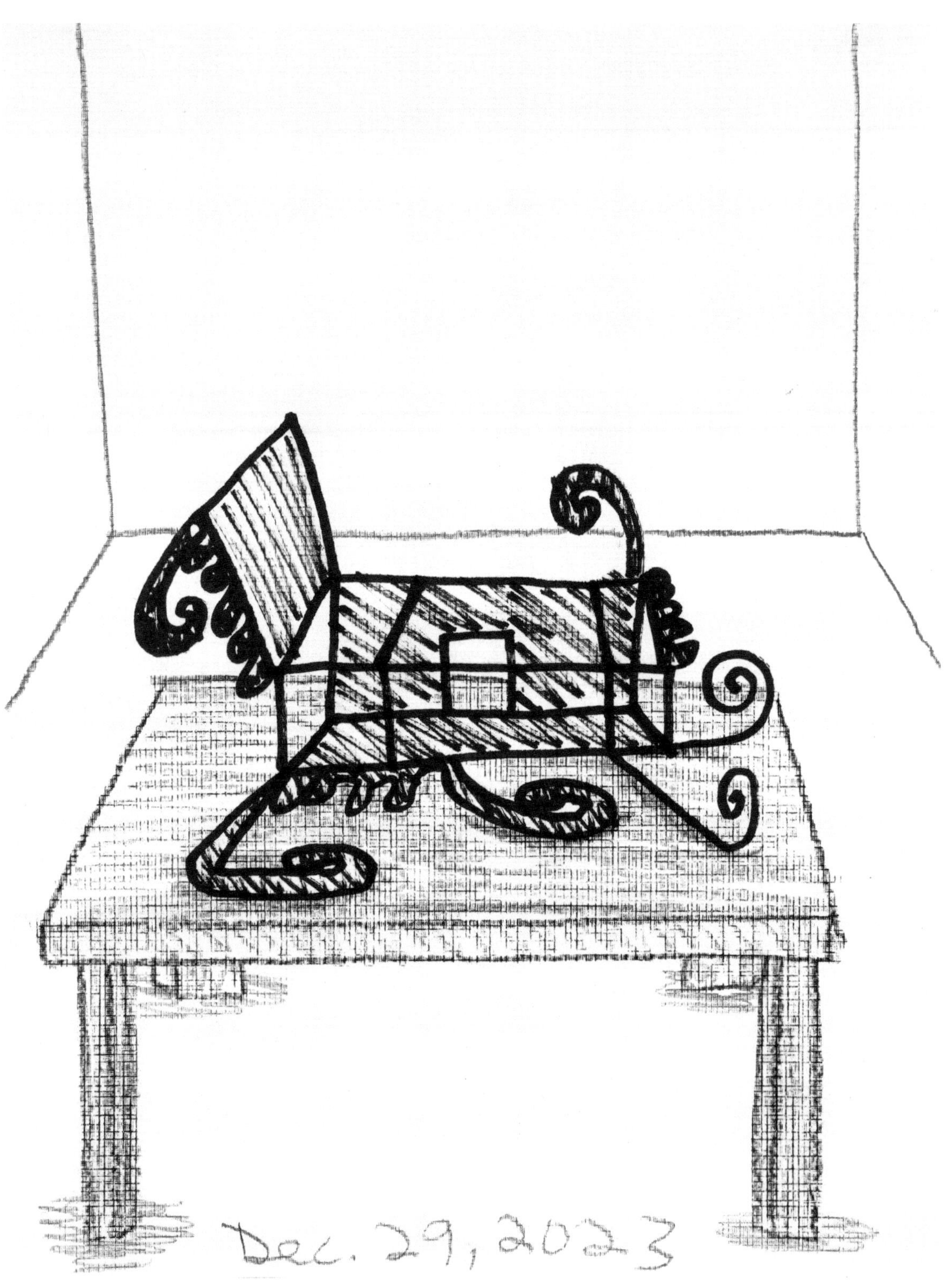

Dec. 29, 2023

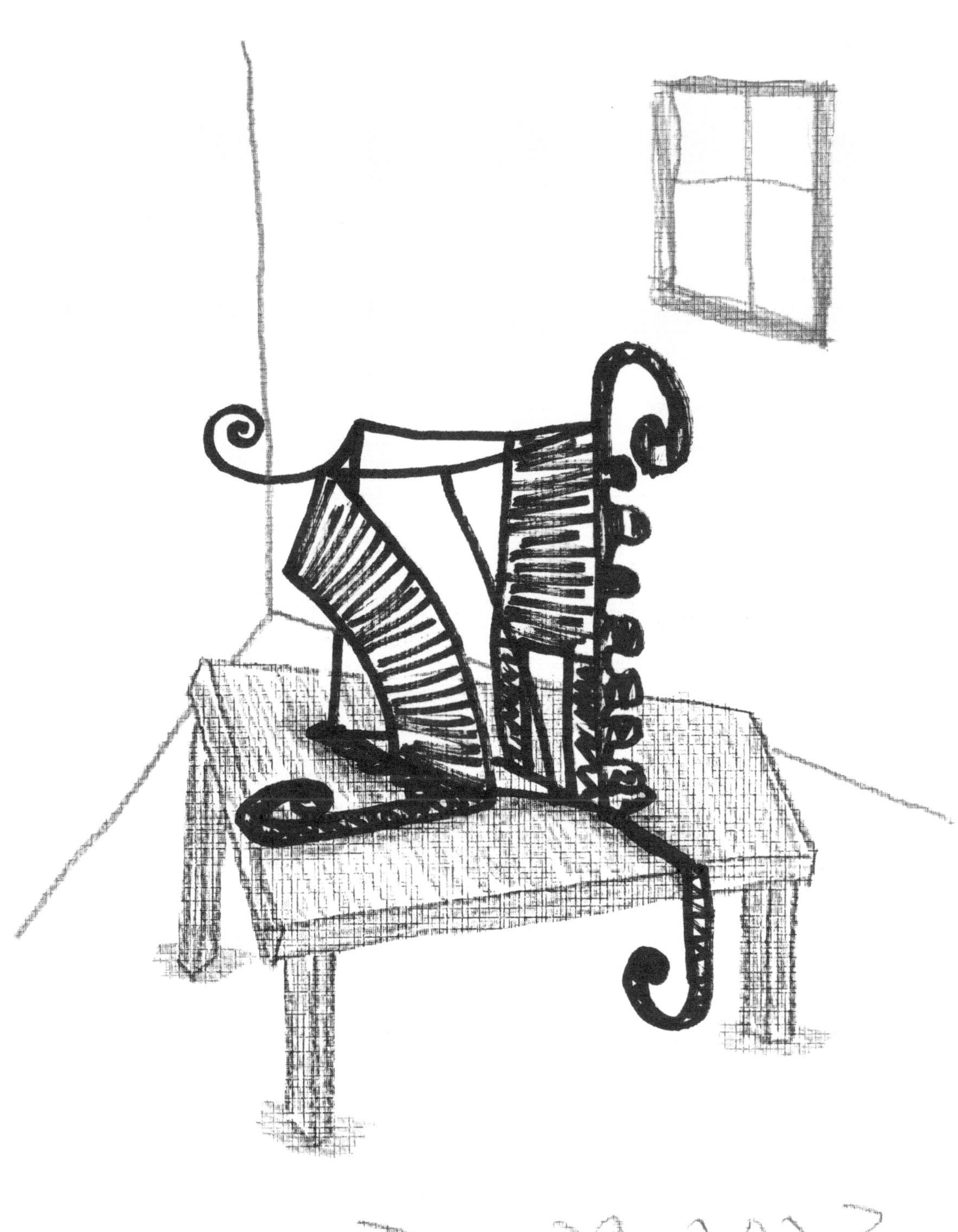

Dec. 29, 2023

1/27/24

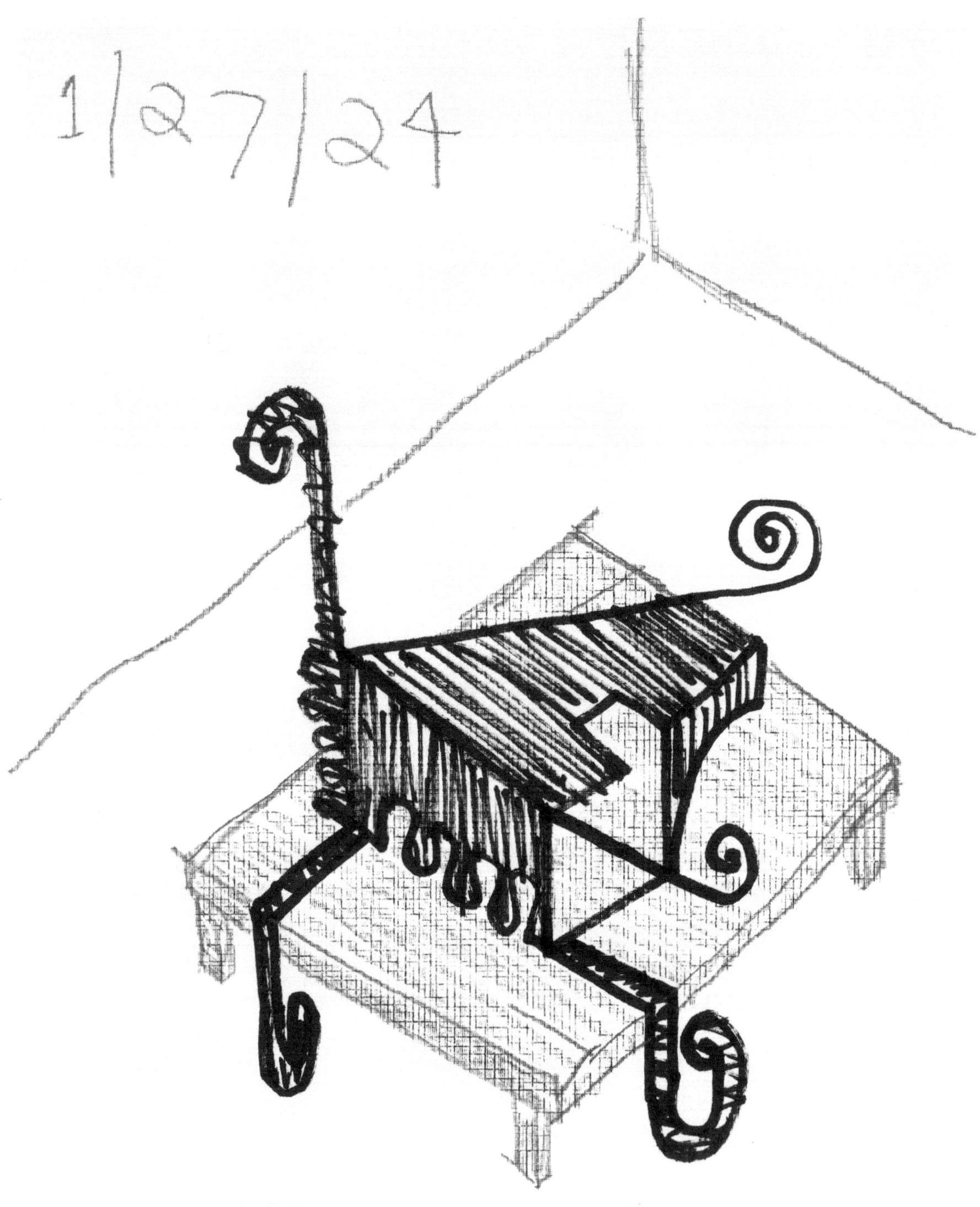

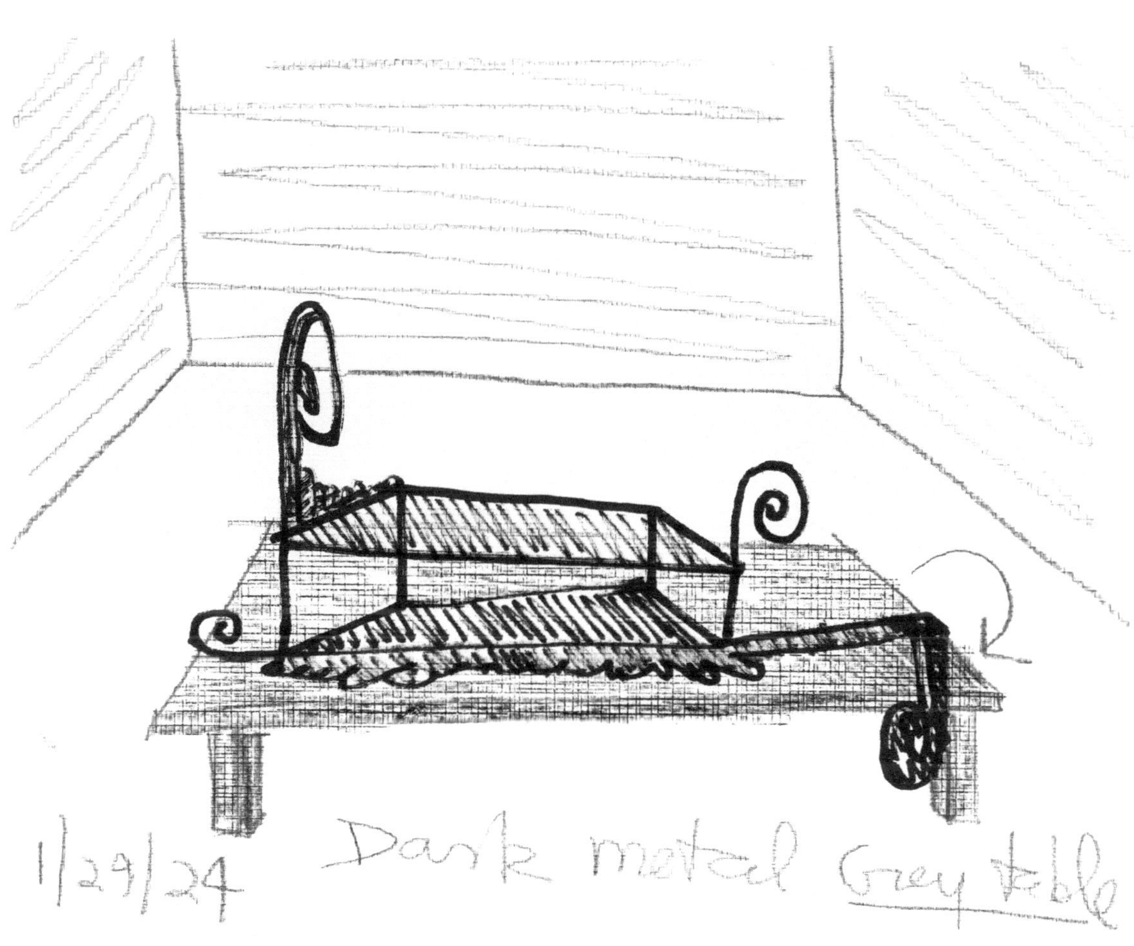

1/29/24 Dark metal Grey table

1/29/24

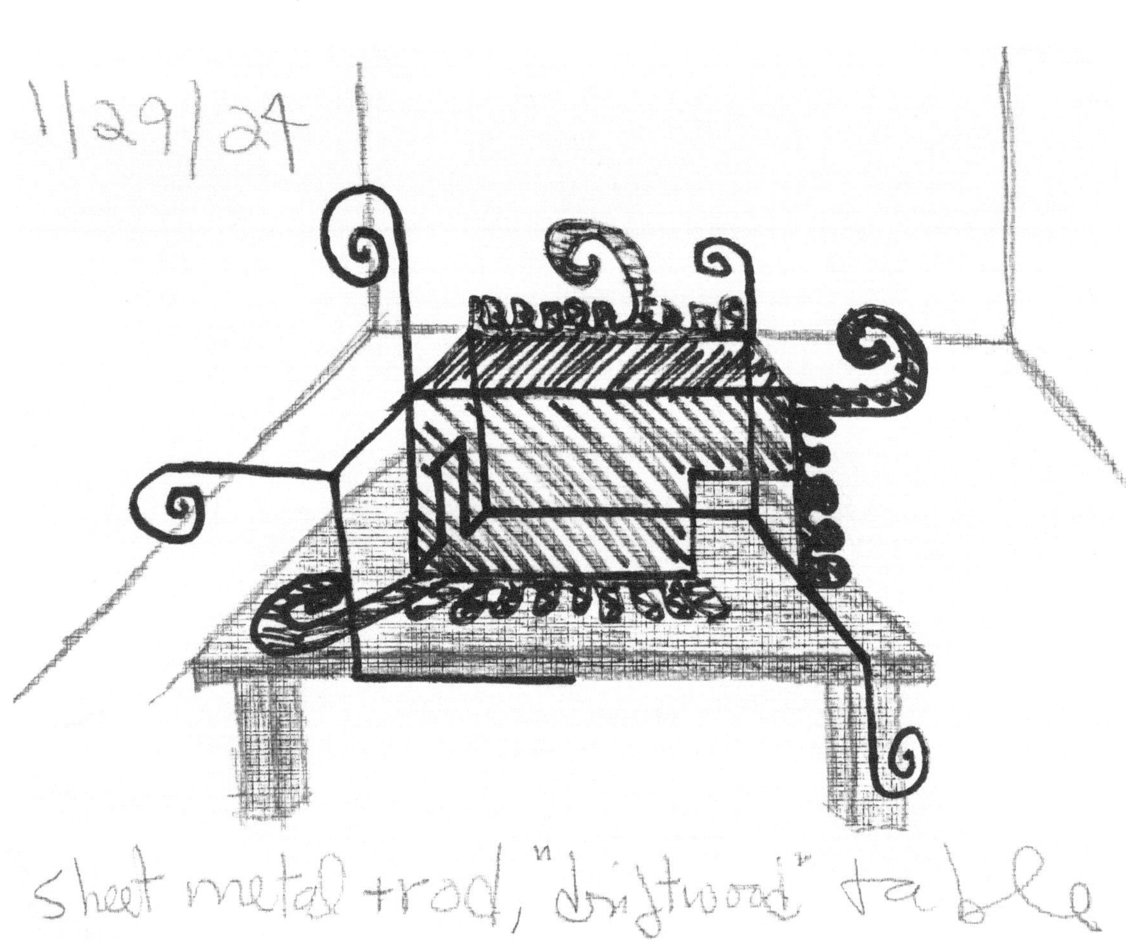

sheet metal trad, "driftwood" table

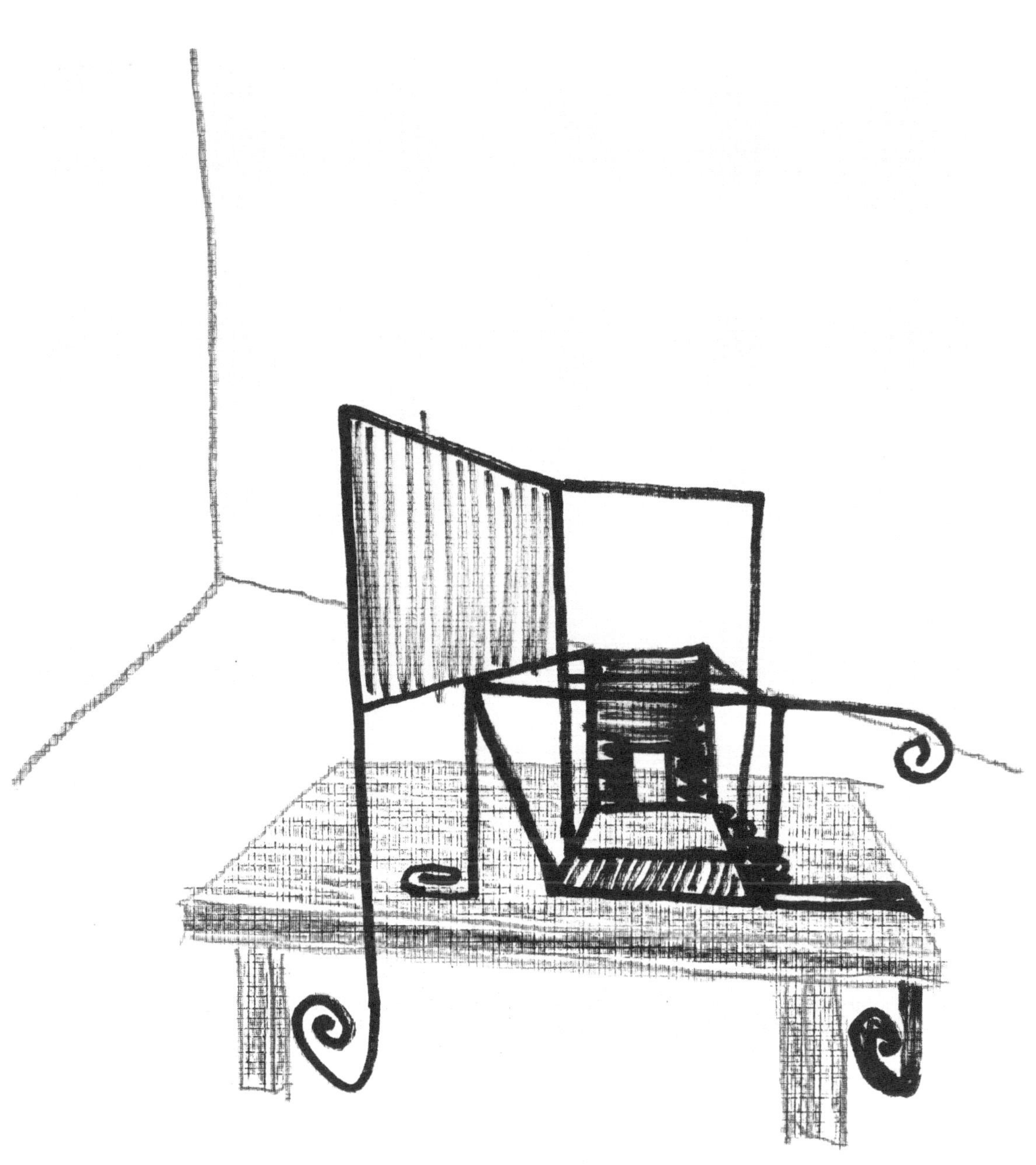

11/20/24

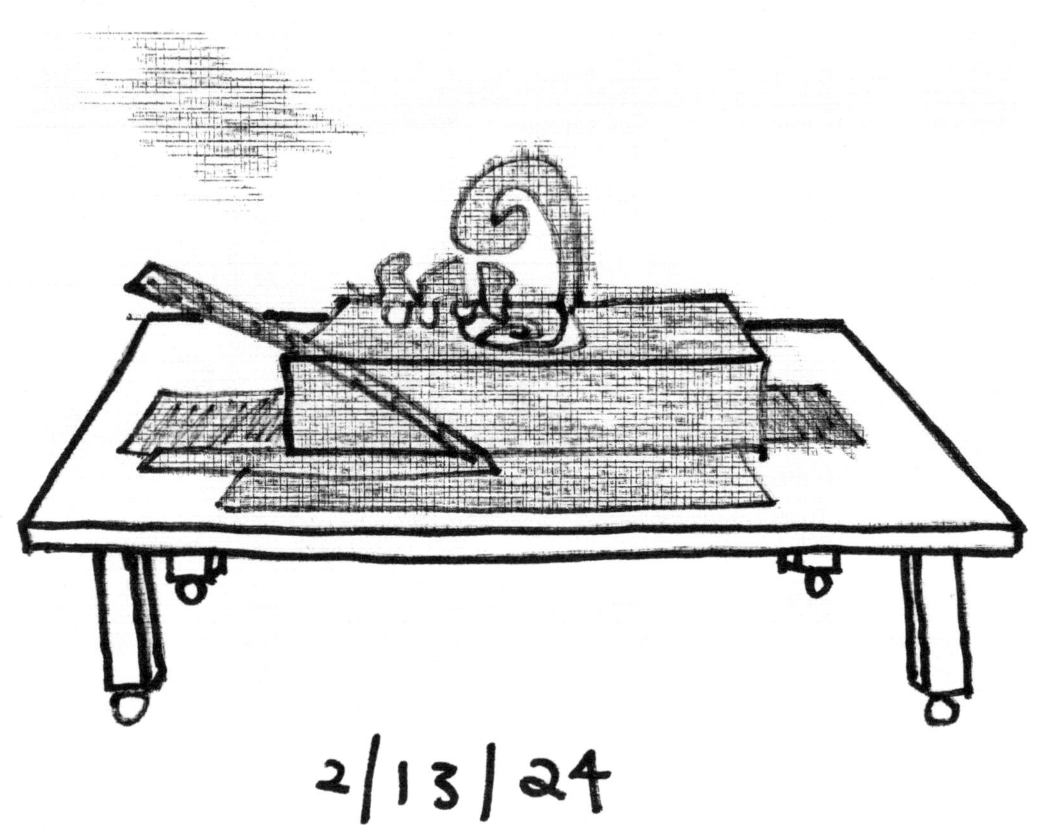

2/13/24

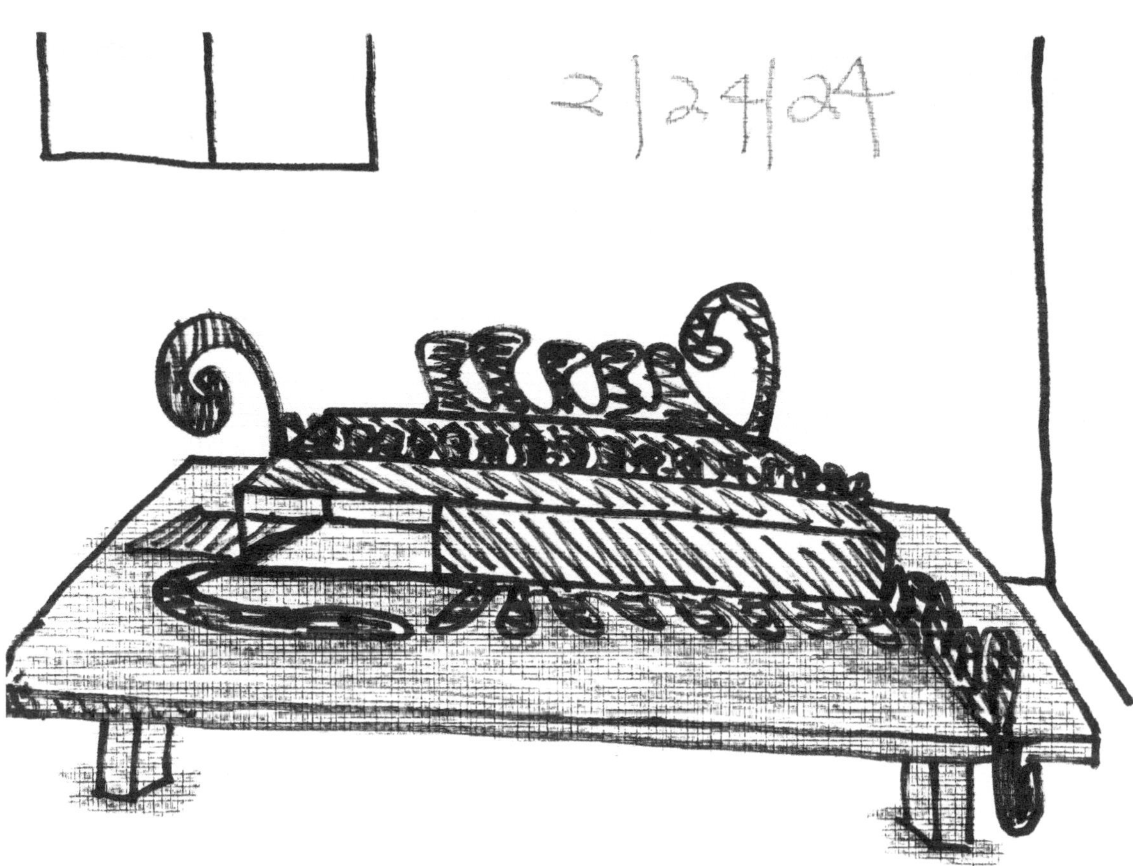

2/24/24

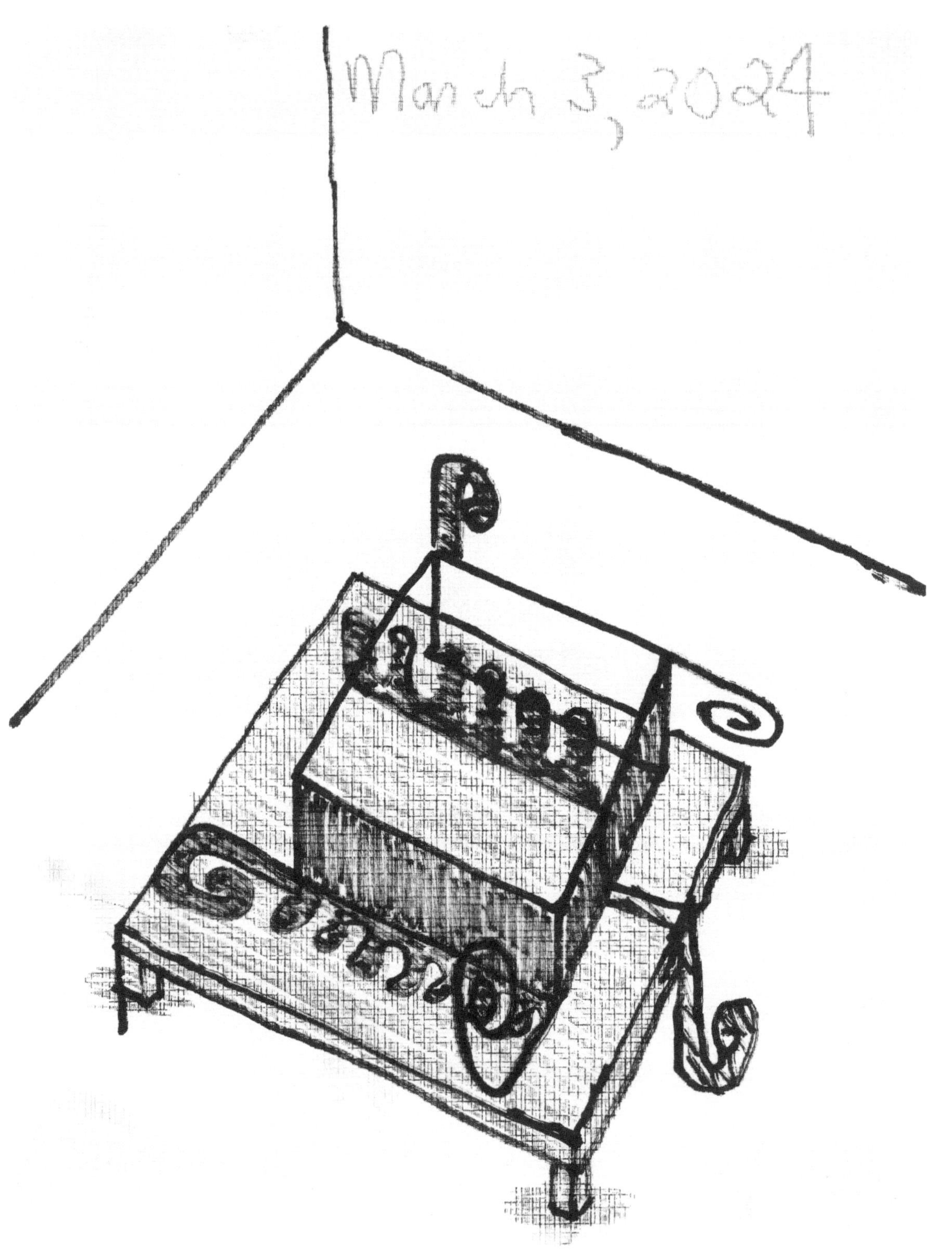

March 3, 2024

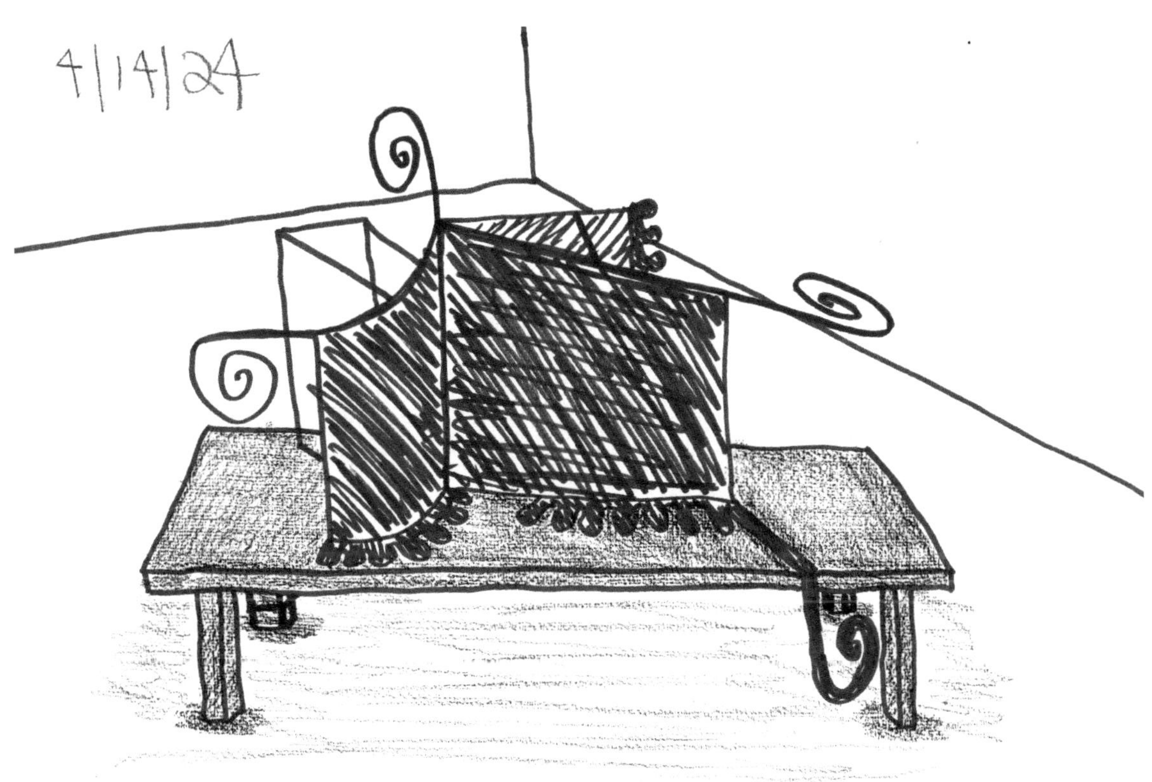
4/14/24

4/14/24

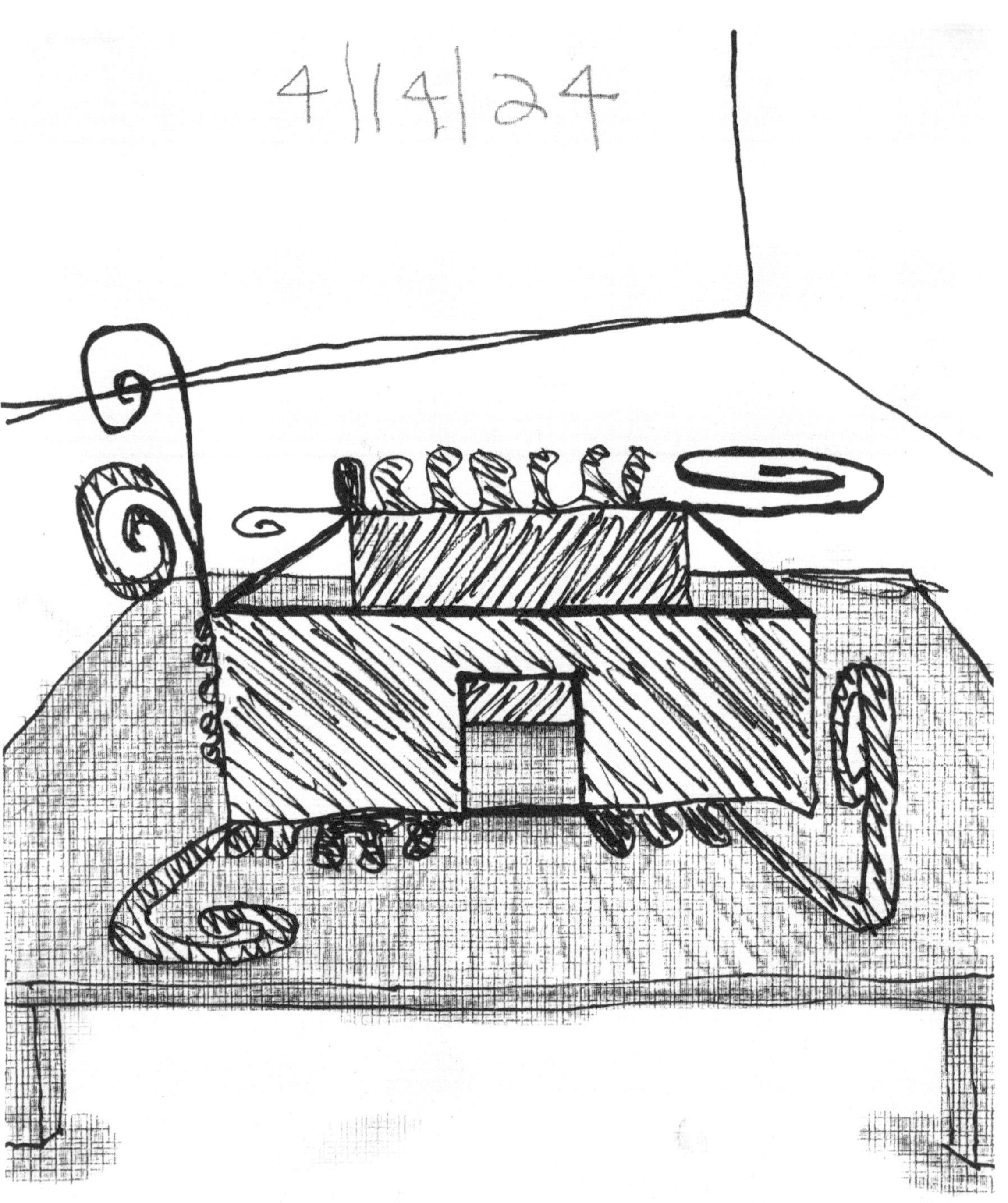

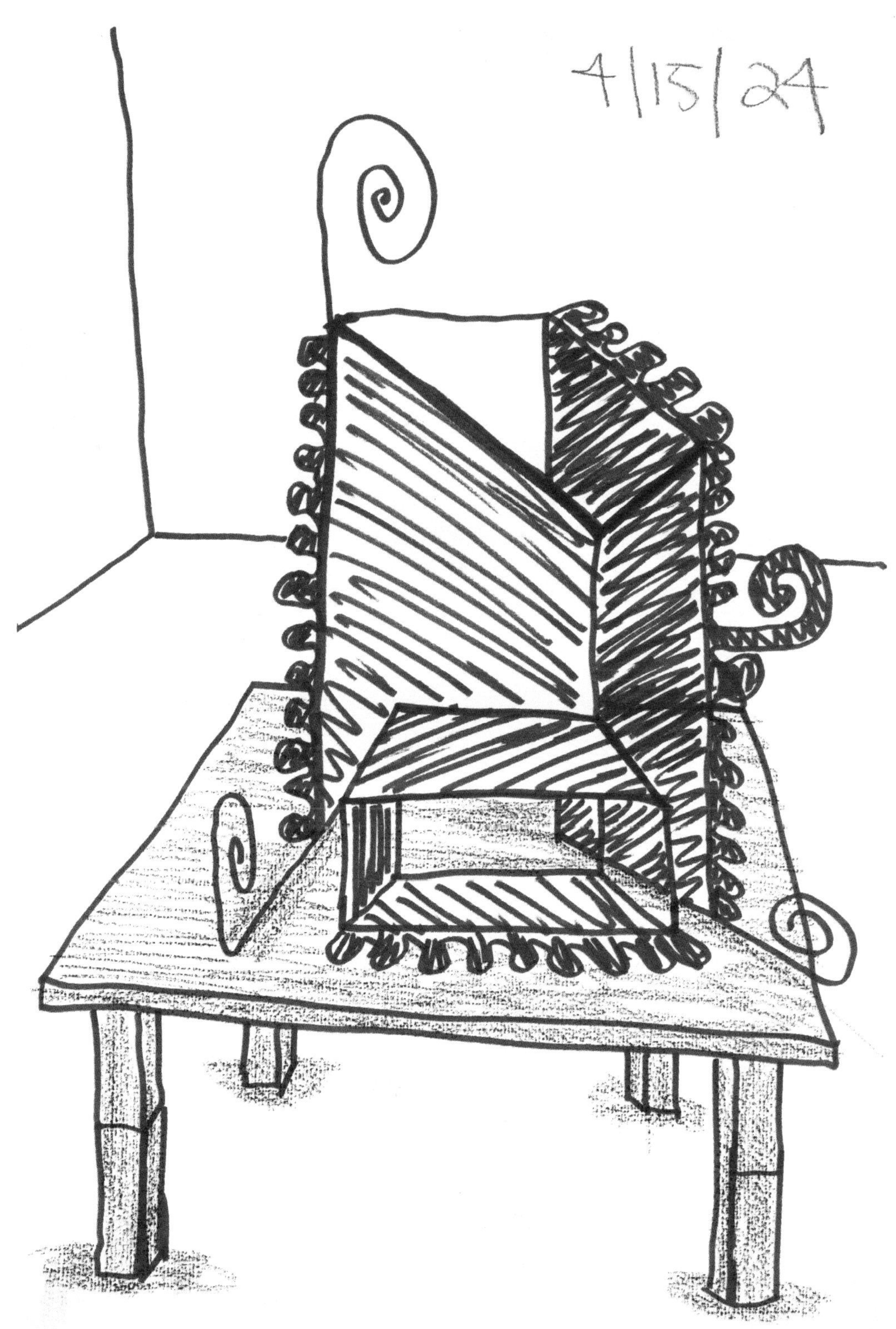

4/15/24

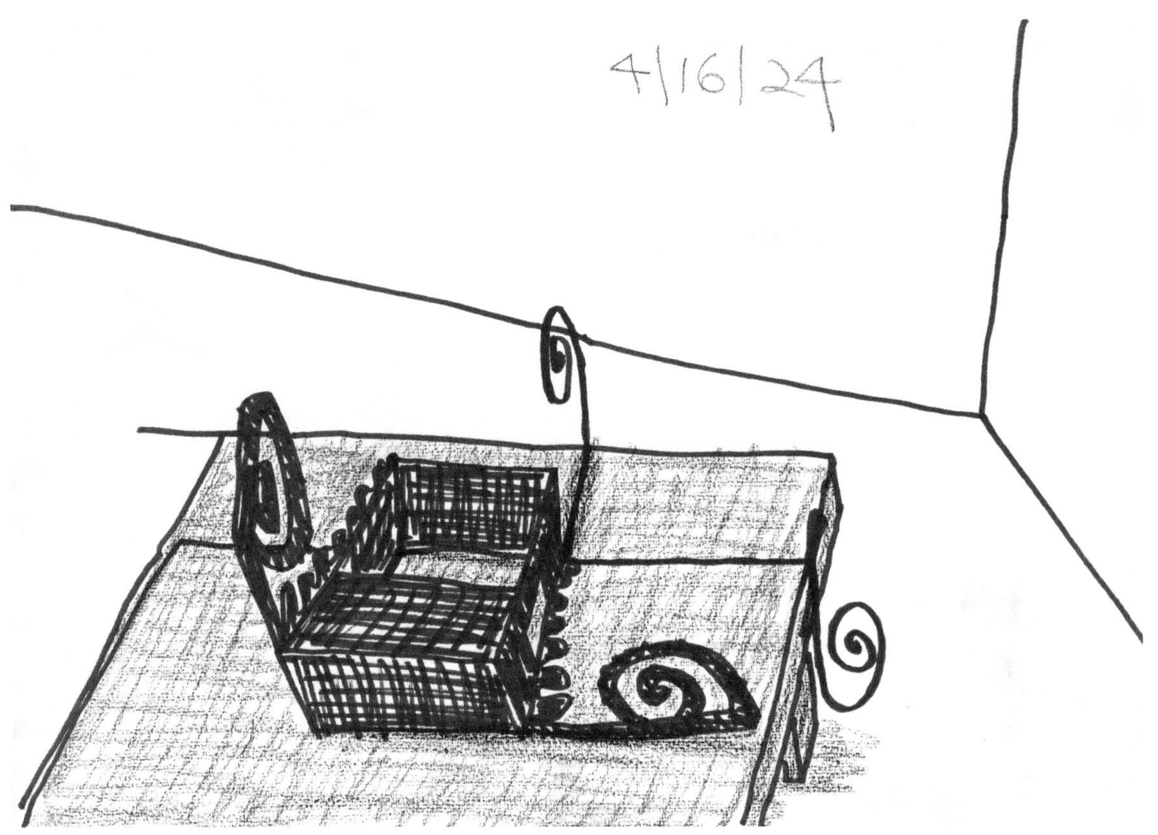
4/16/24

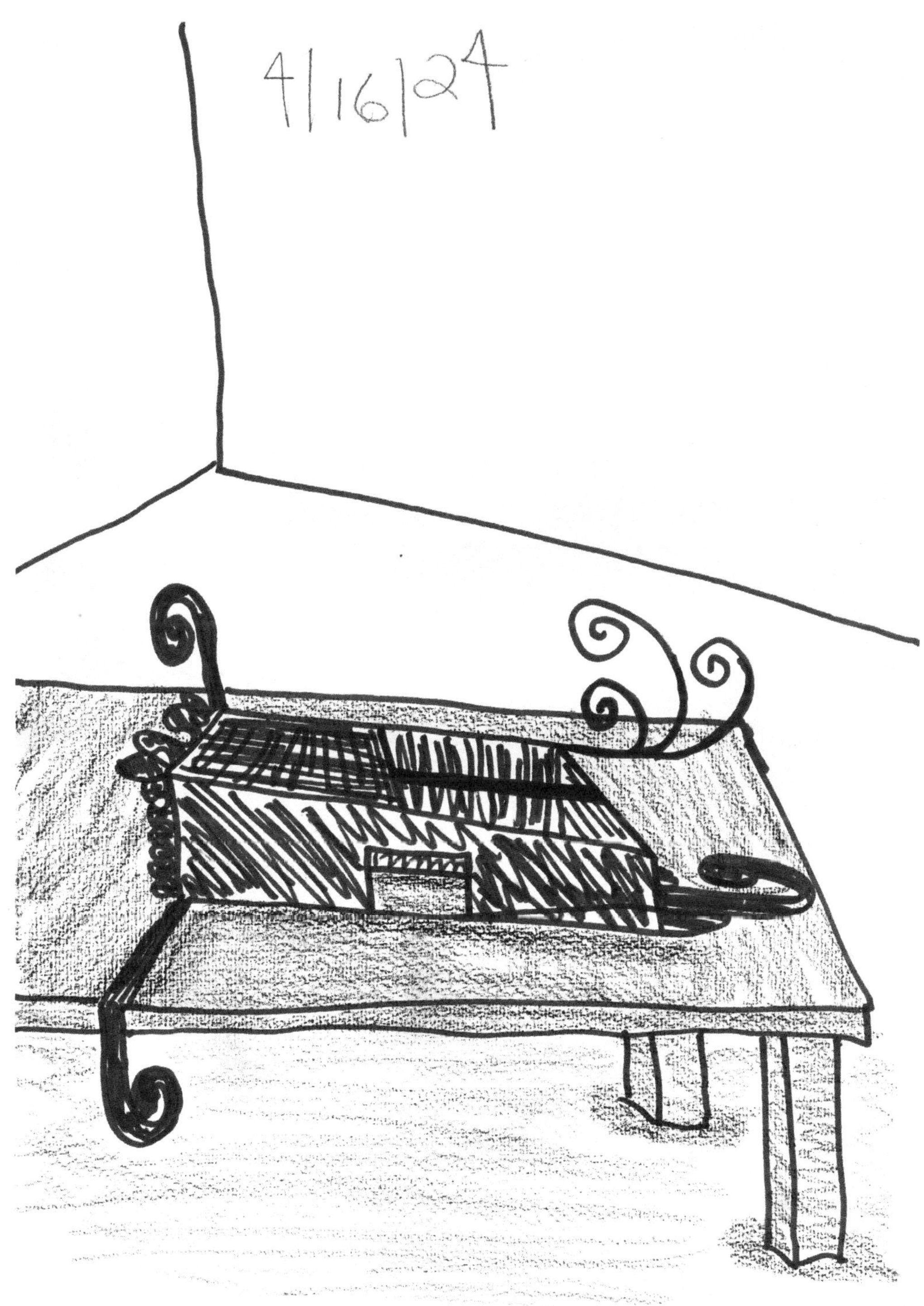

4/16/24

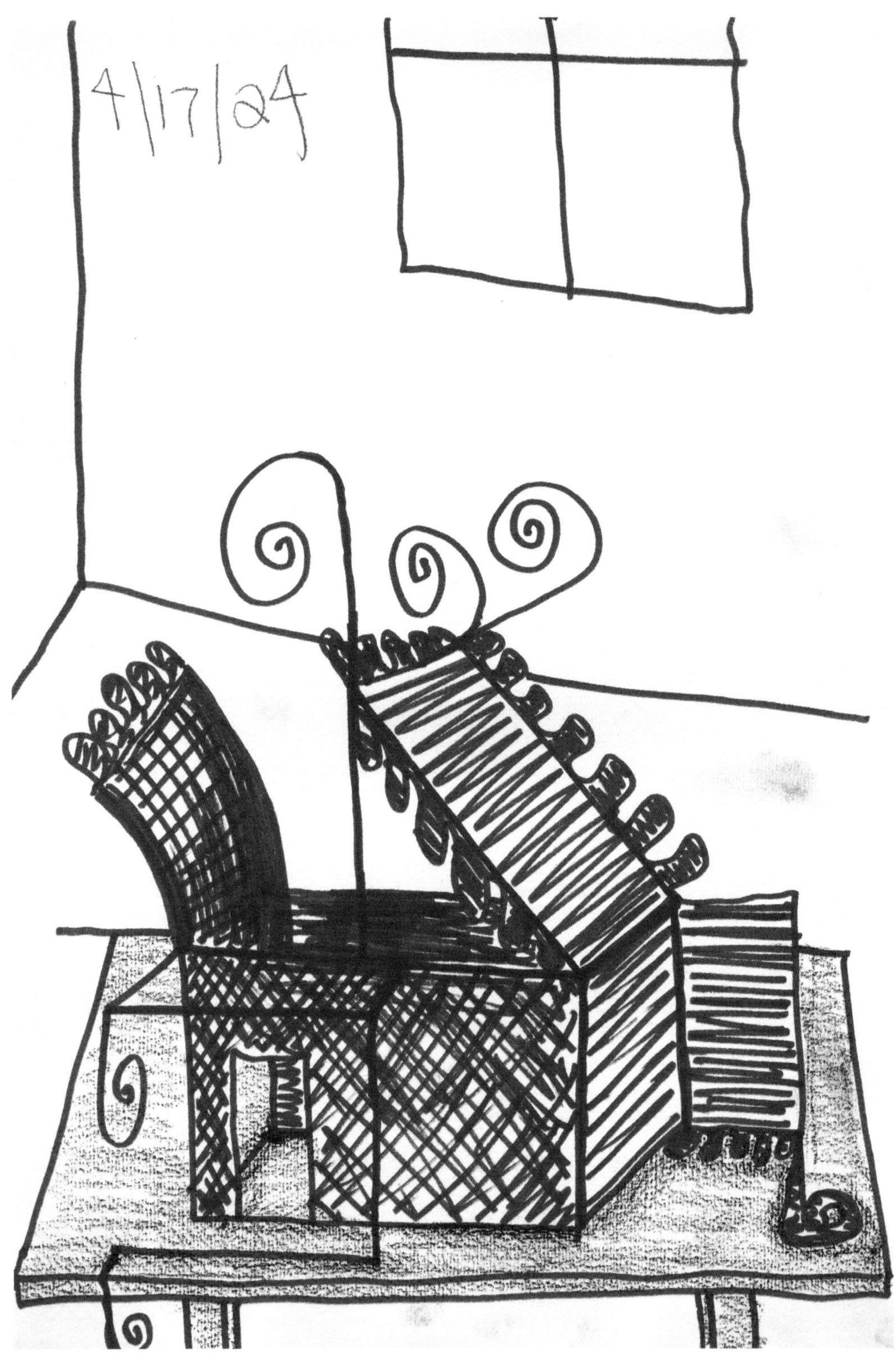

4/17/24

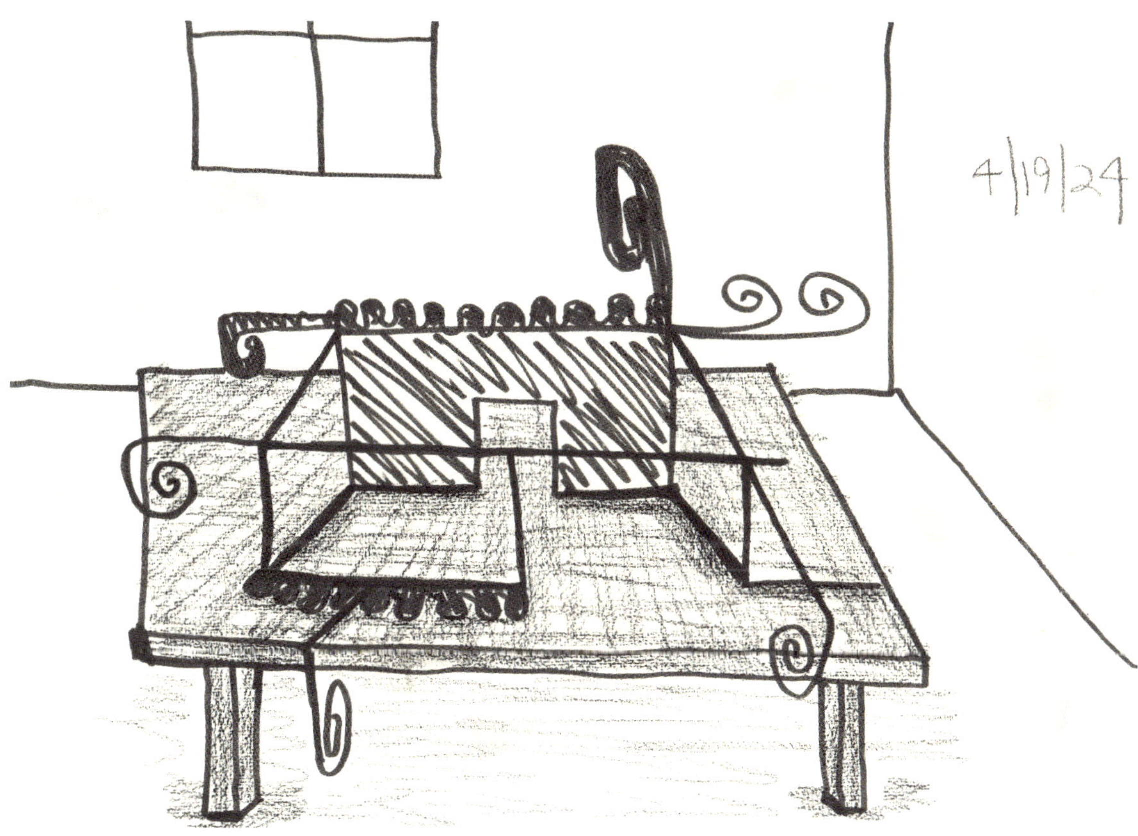

4/19/24

4| 23| 24

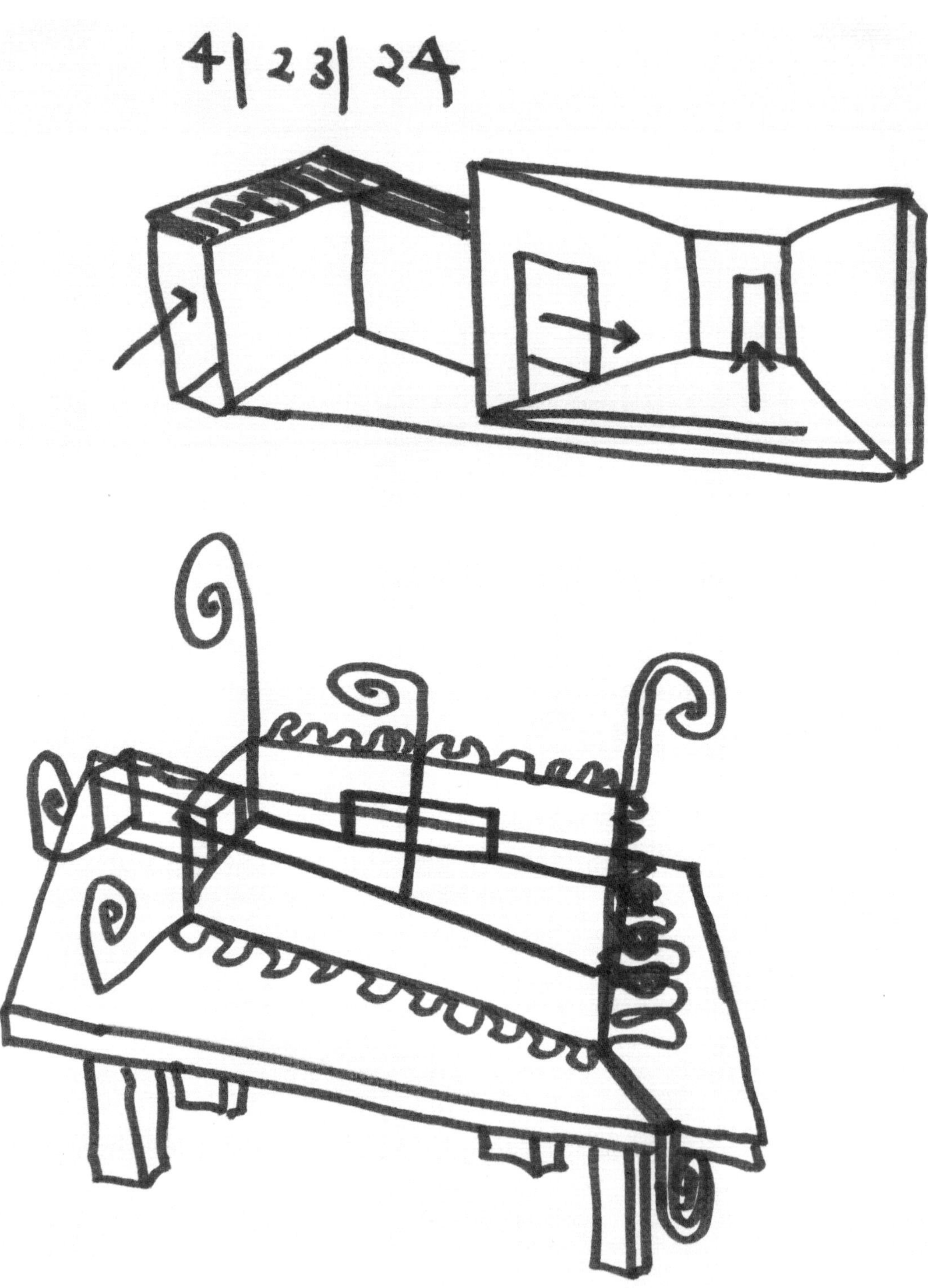

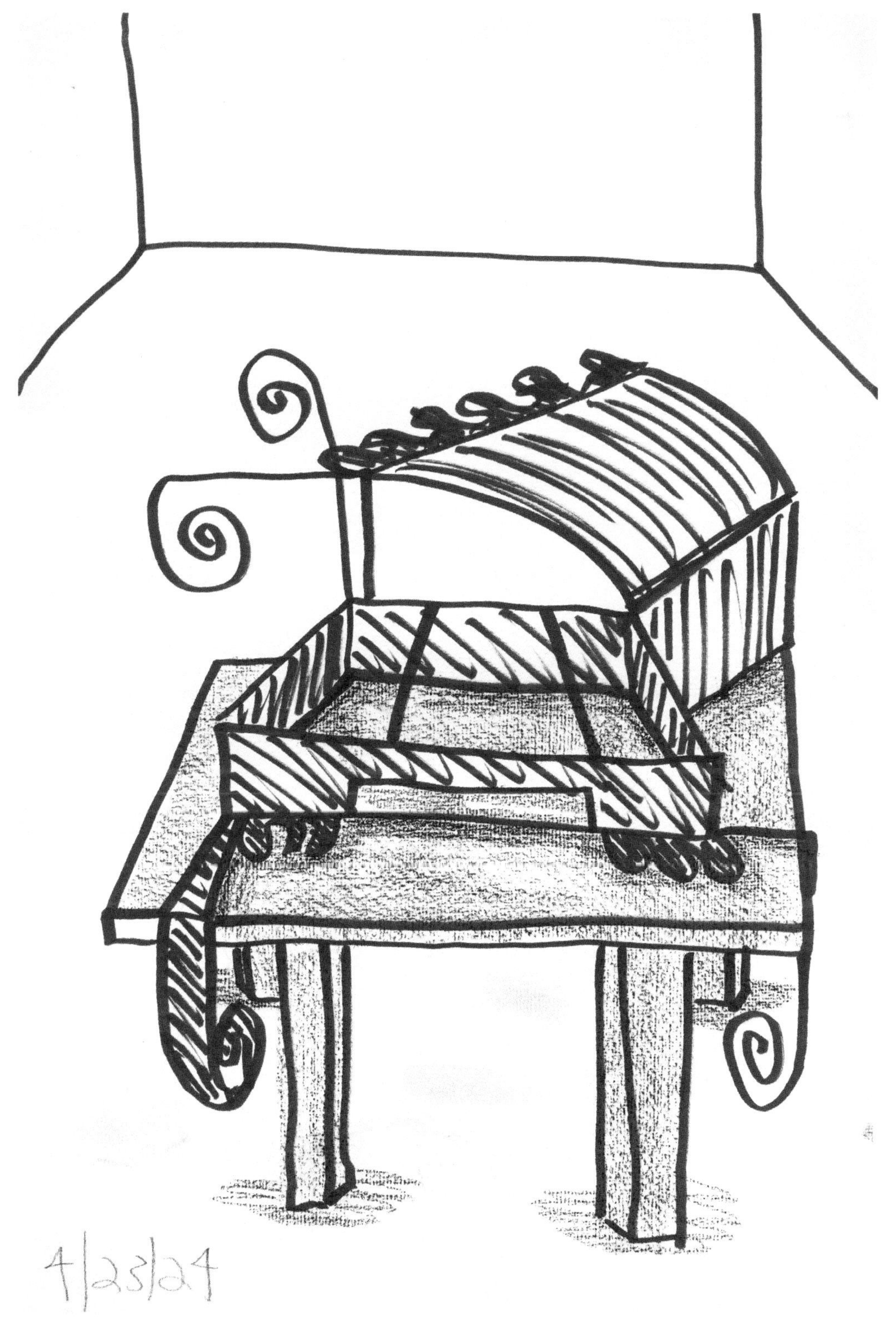

7/25/24

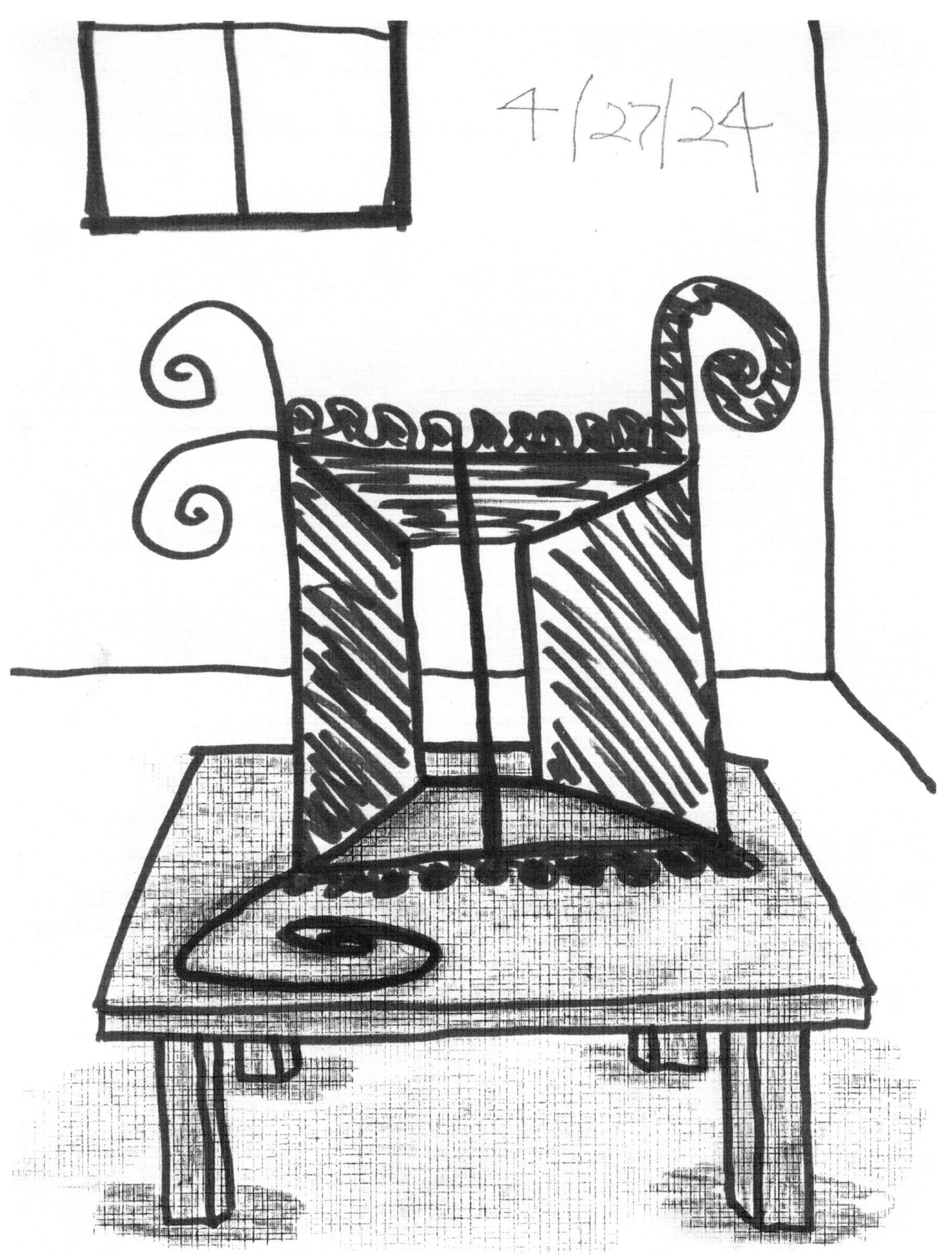
4/27/24

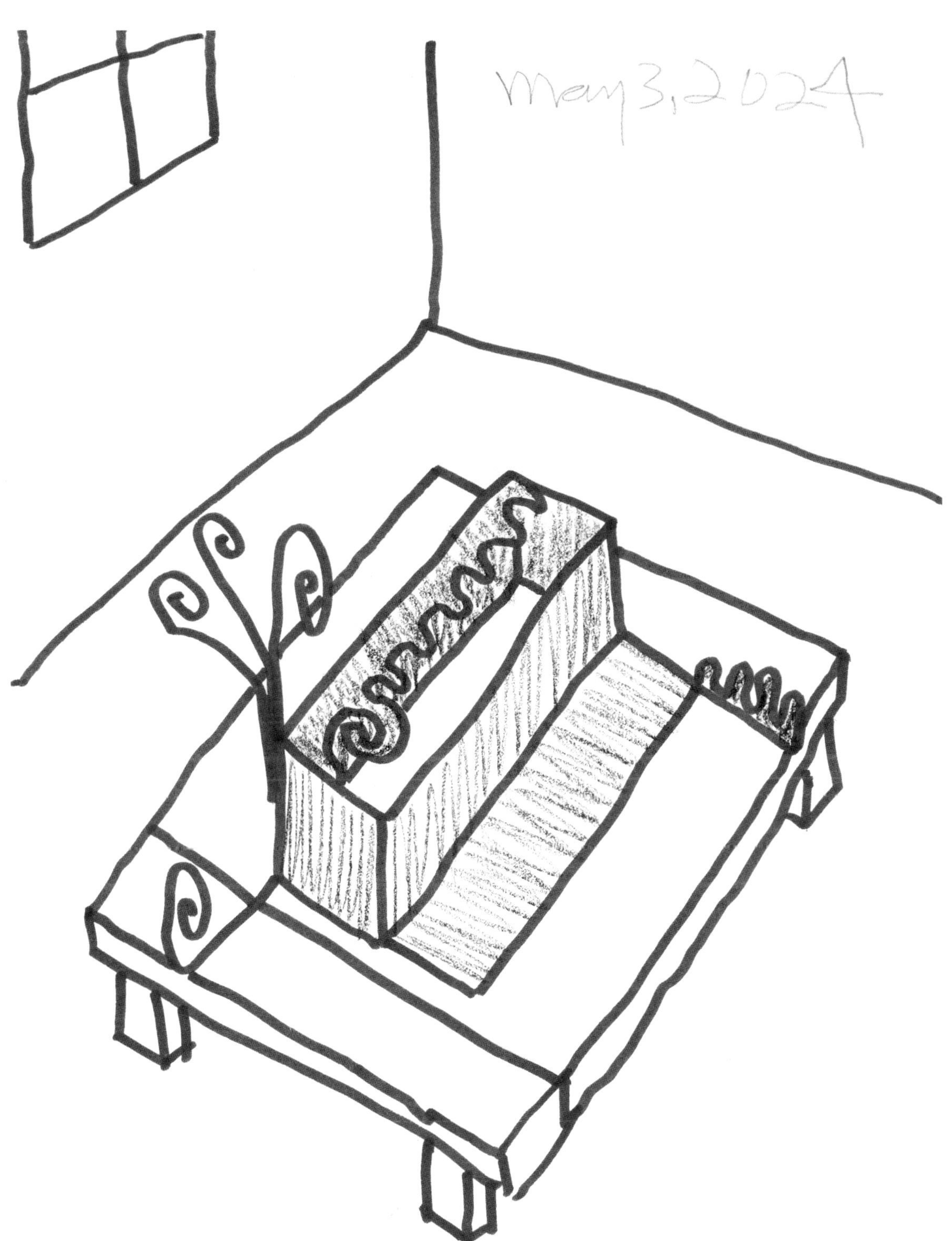

may 3, 2024

5/18/24

Anything attached to
anything & everything

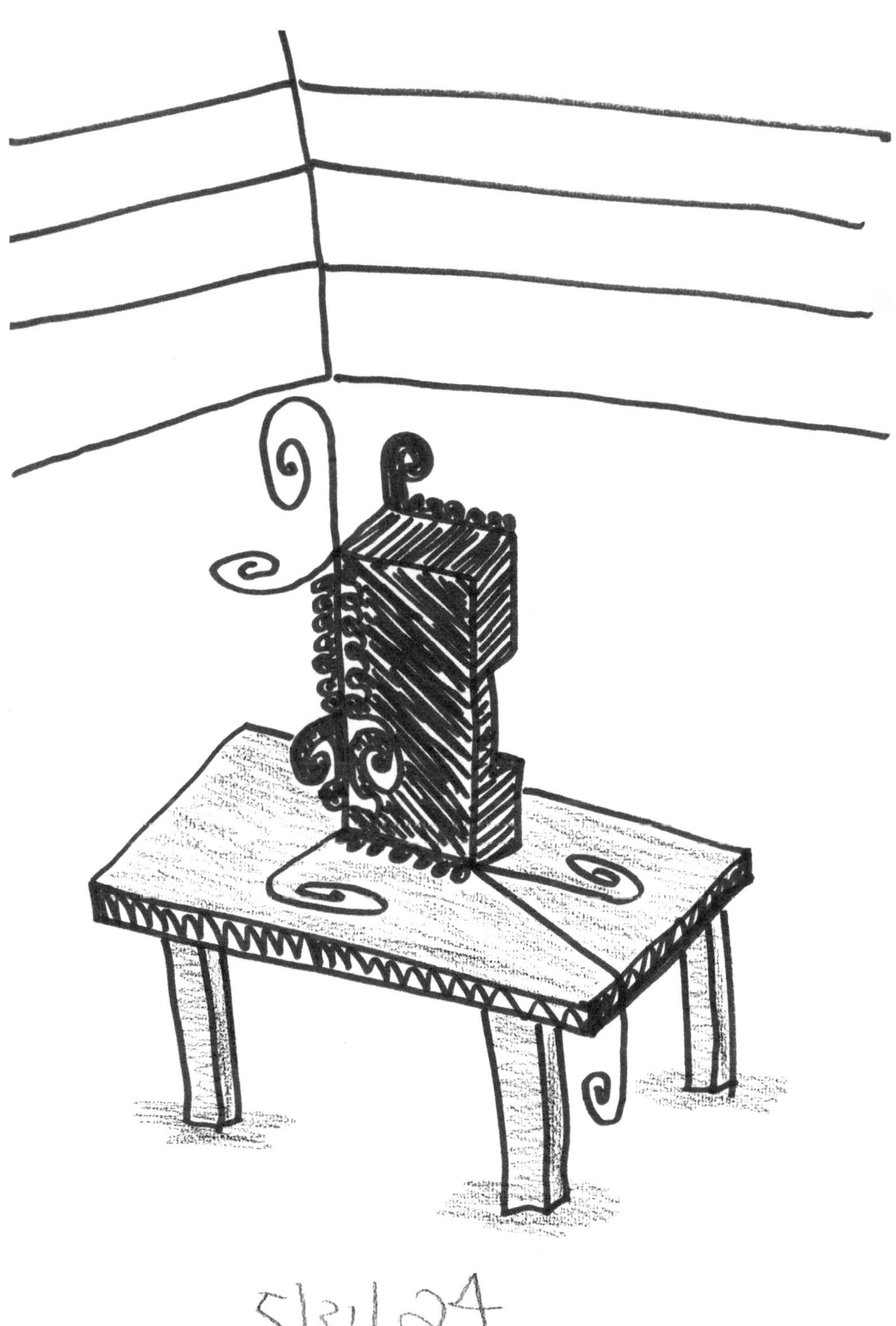

5/31/24

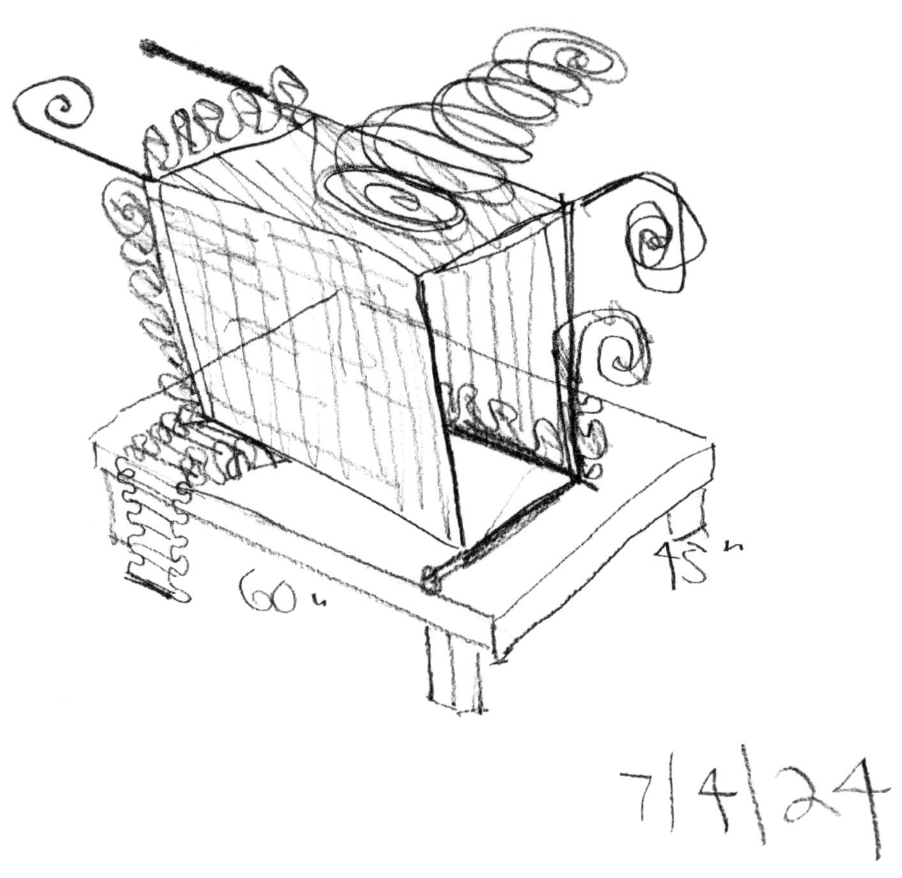

60"
75"
7/4/24

Black box

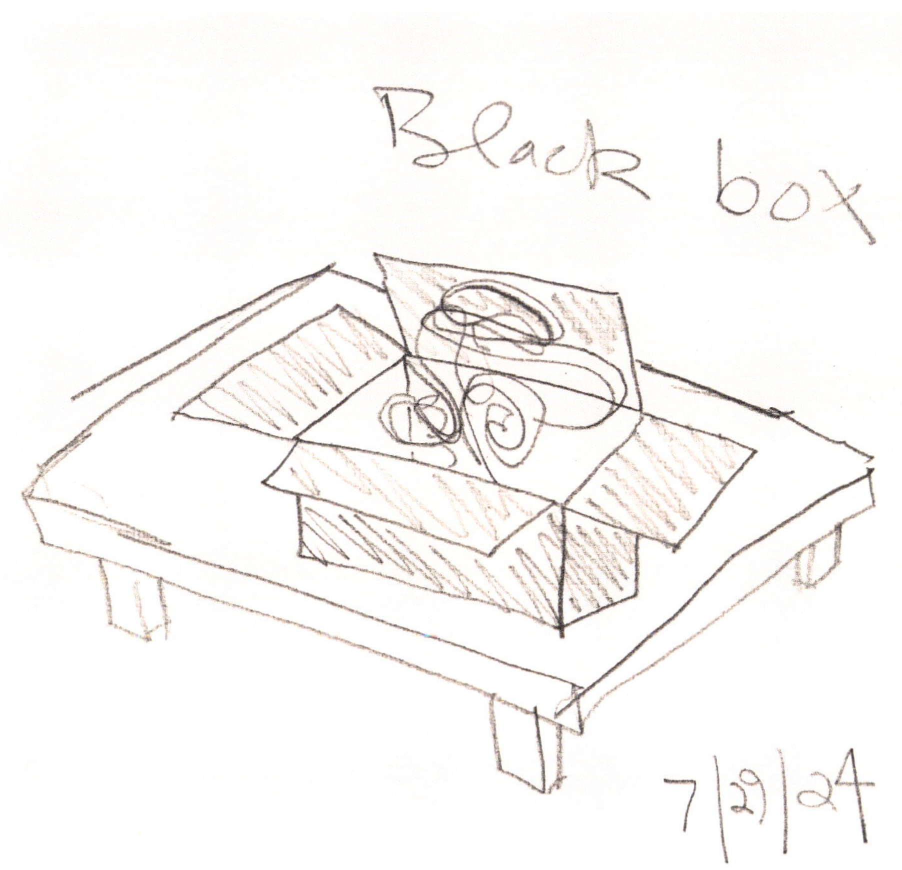

7/29/24

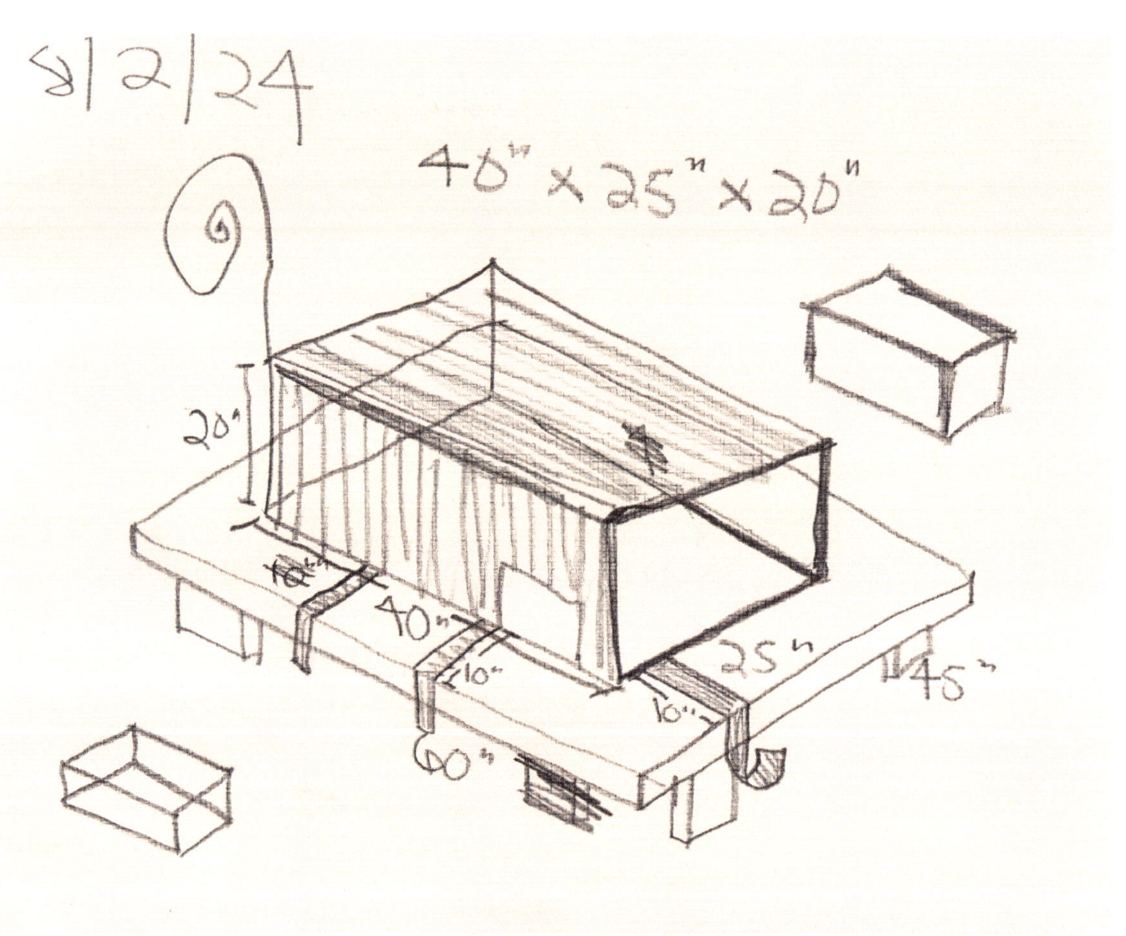
8/2/24
40" x 25" x 20"
20"
40"
25"
45"
10"
10"
20"
10"

8/2/24
8/3/24

Black Box 3

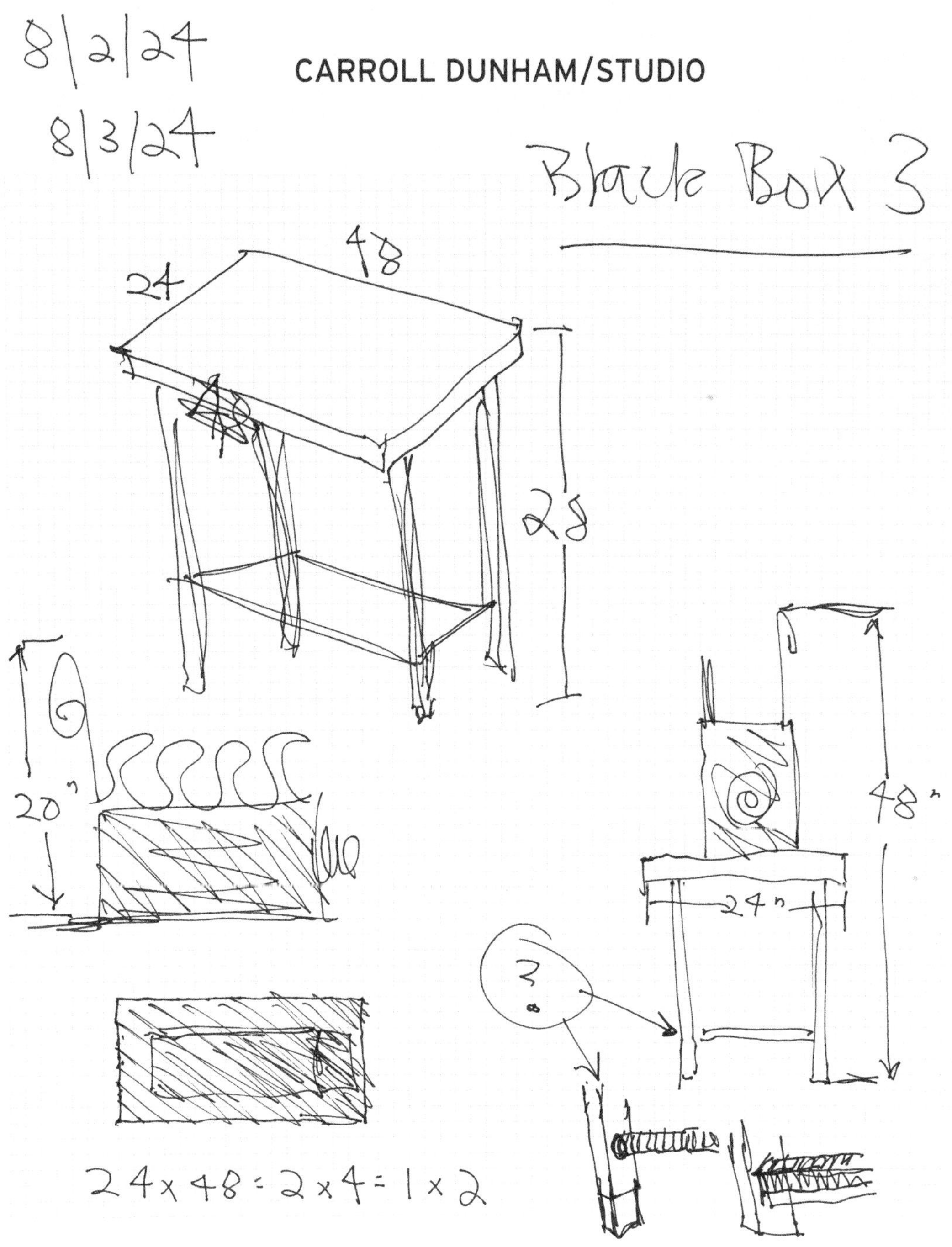

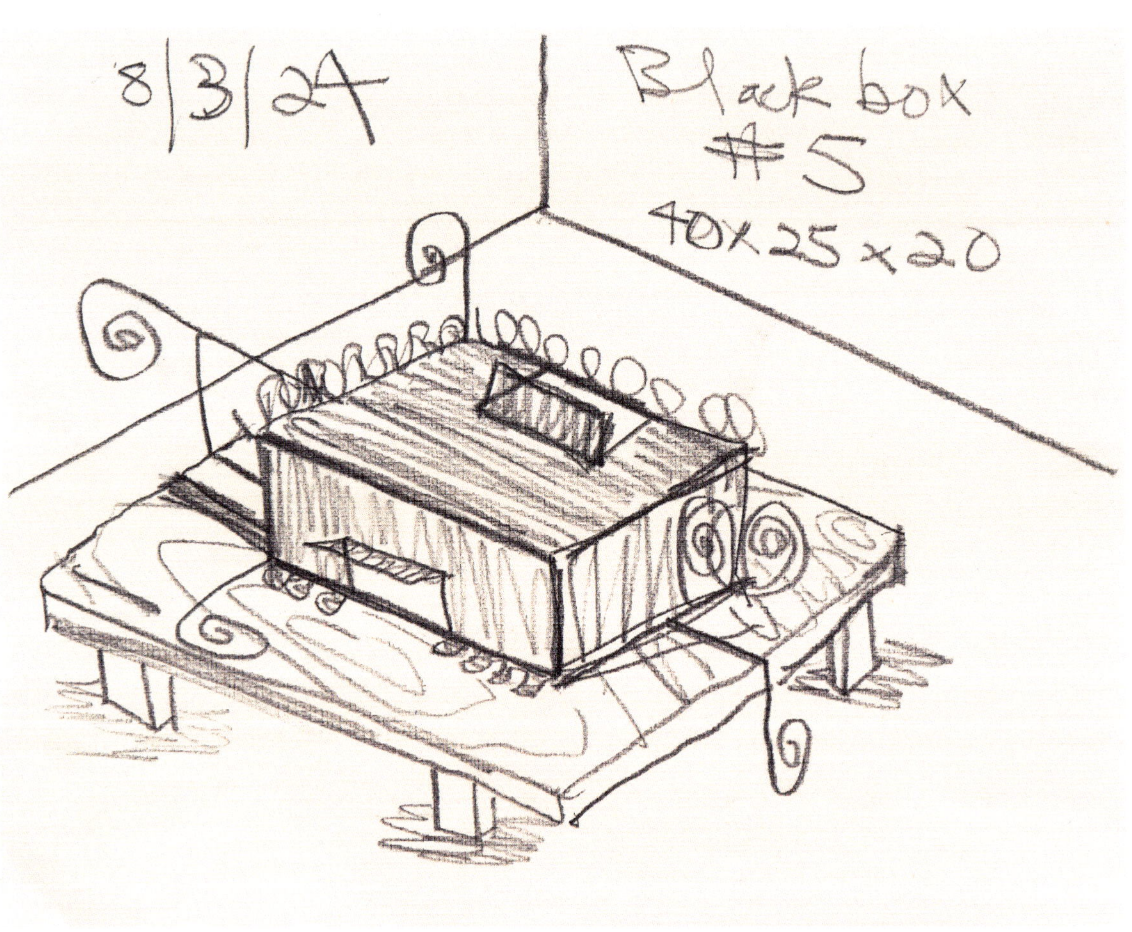

8/3/24
Black box
#5
40x25x20

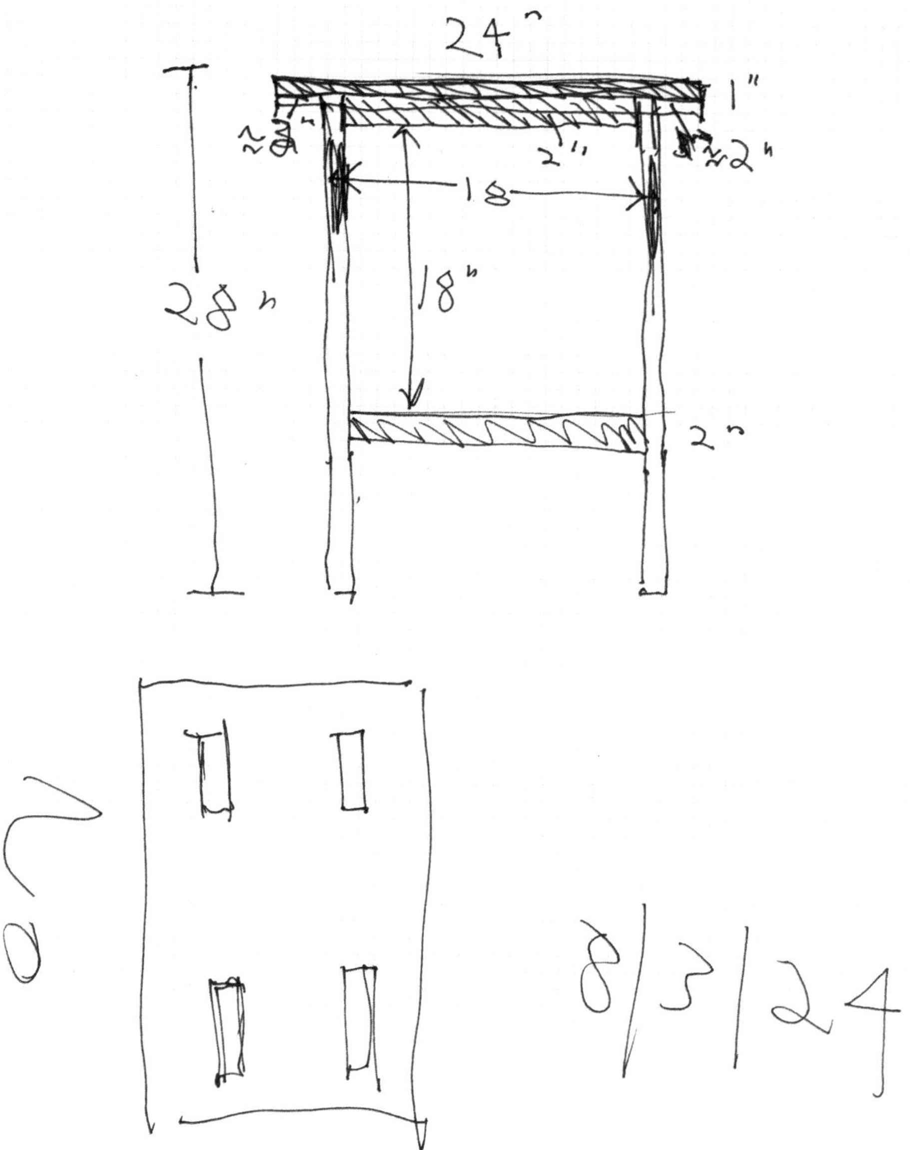

24"
1"
~3/8"
~2"
2"
18
18"
28"
2"
2"
8/3/24

Black Box 5

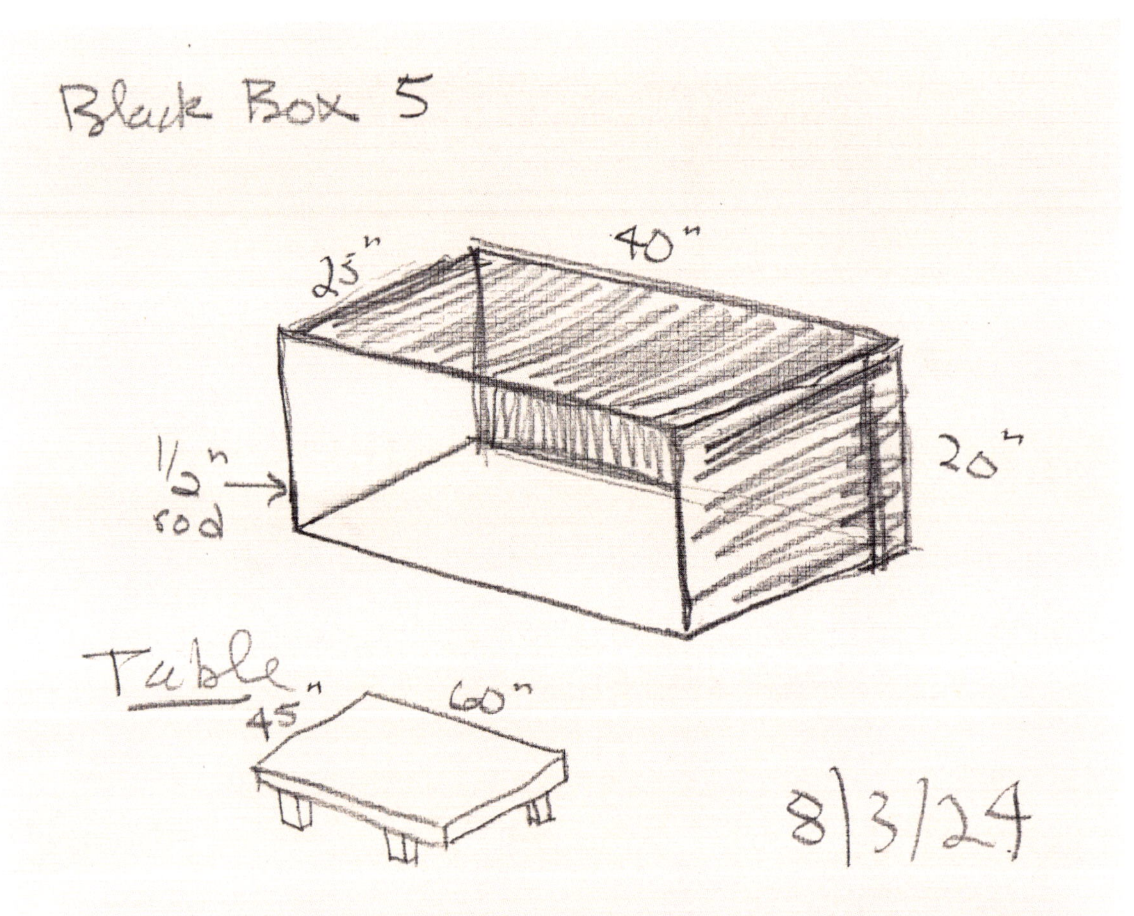

Table
45"
60"

8/3/24

8/5/24

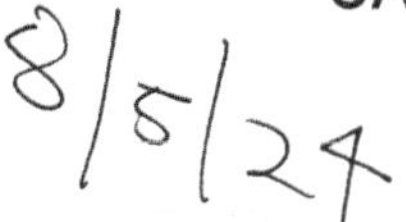

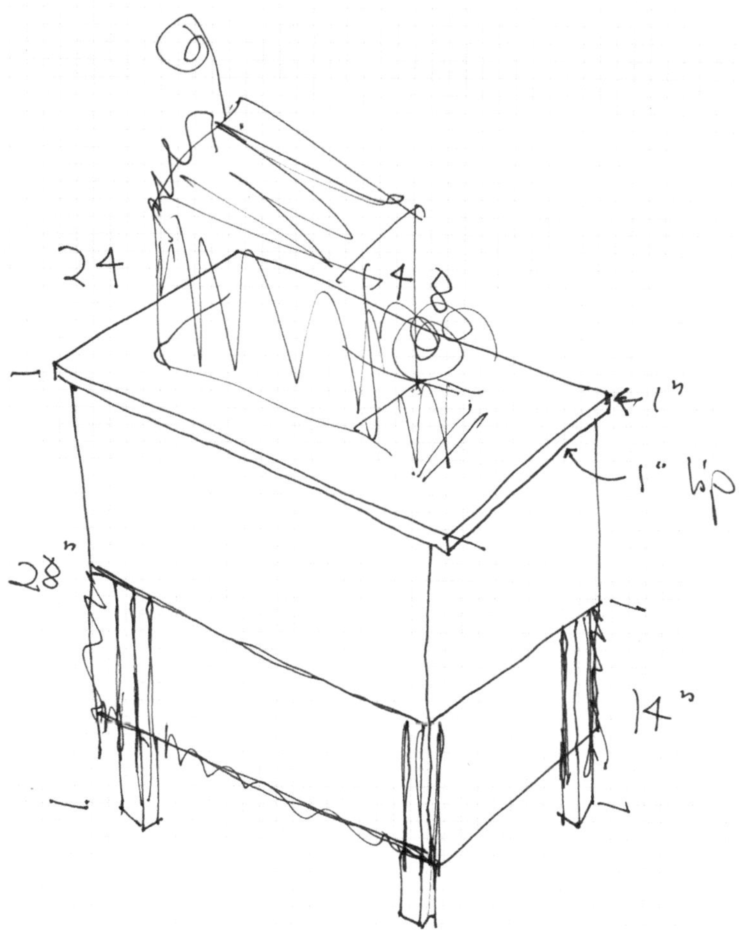

8/6/24

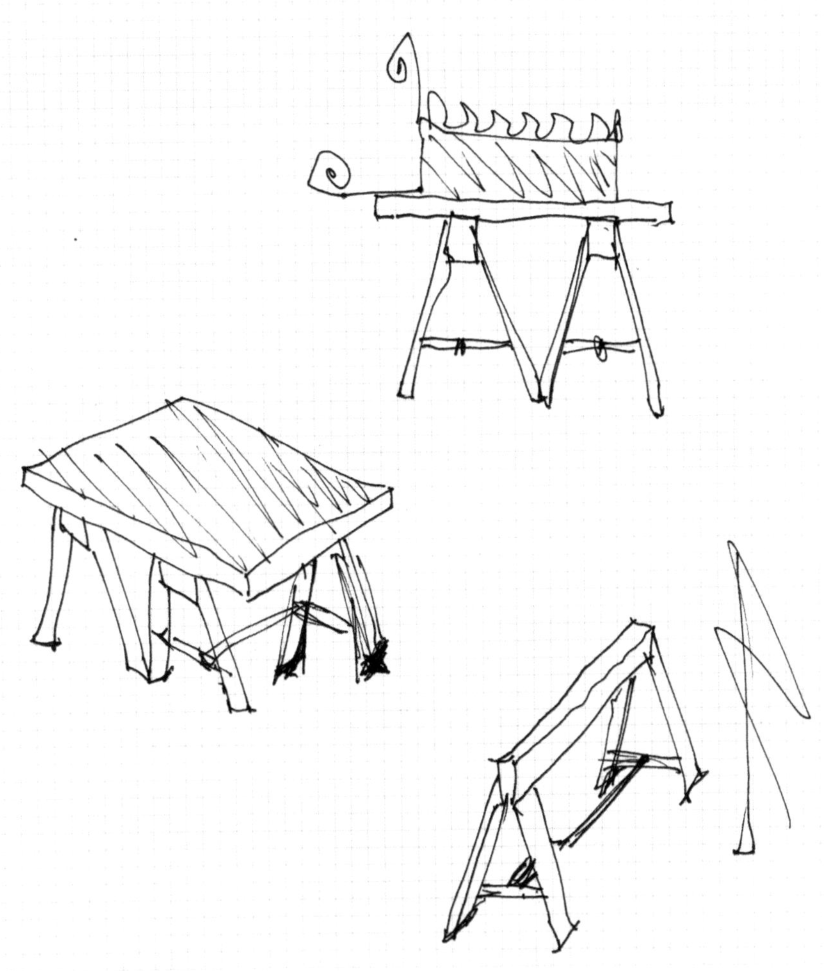

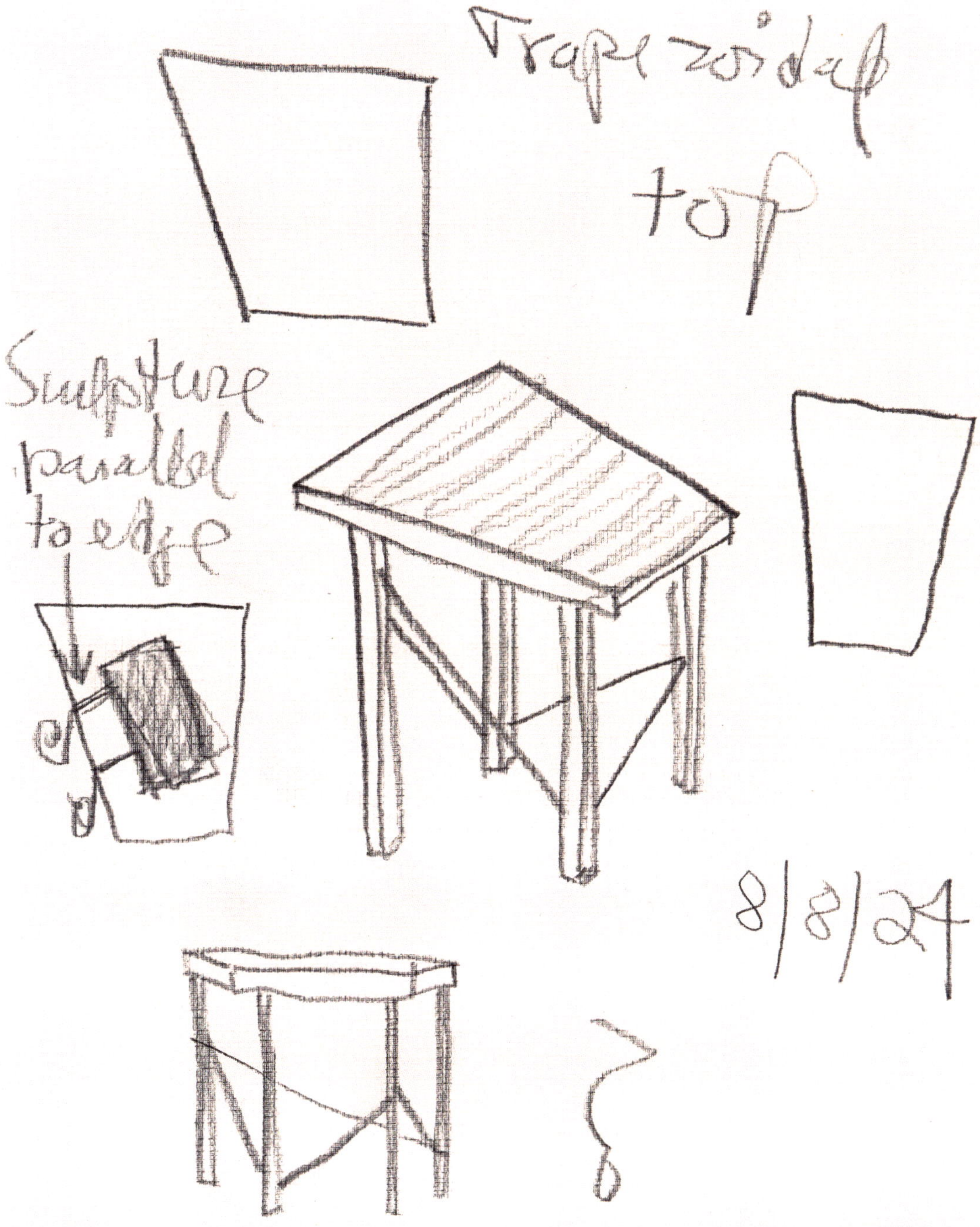

Trapezoidal top

Sculpture parallel to edge

8/8/27

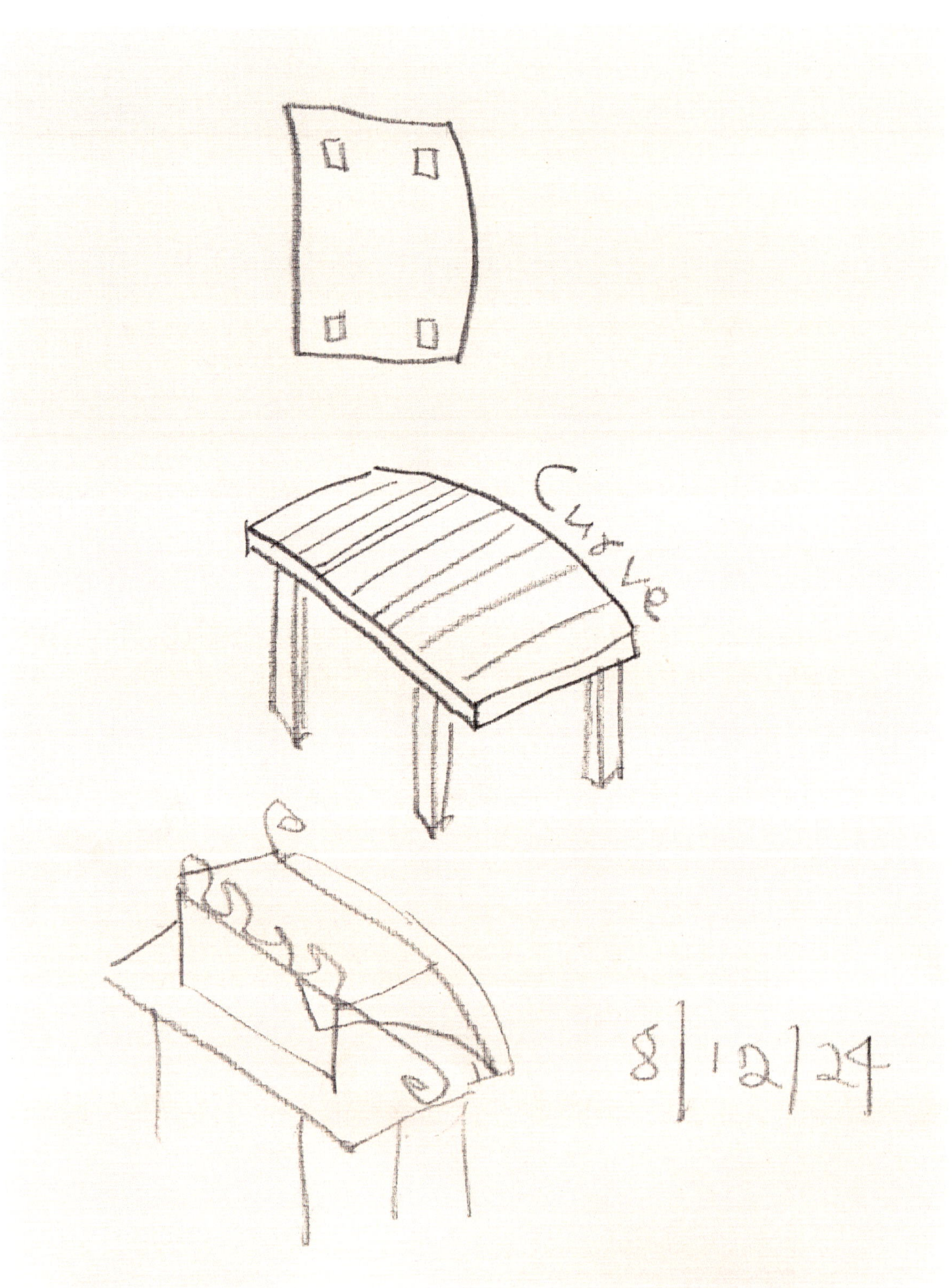

Curve
8/12/24

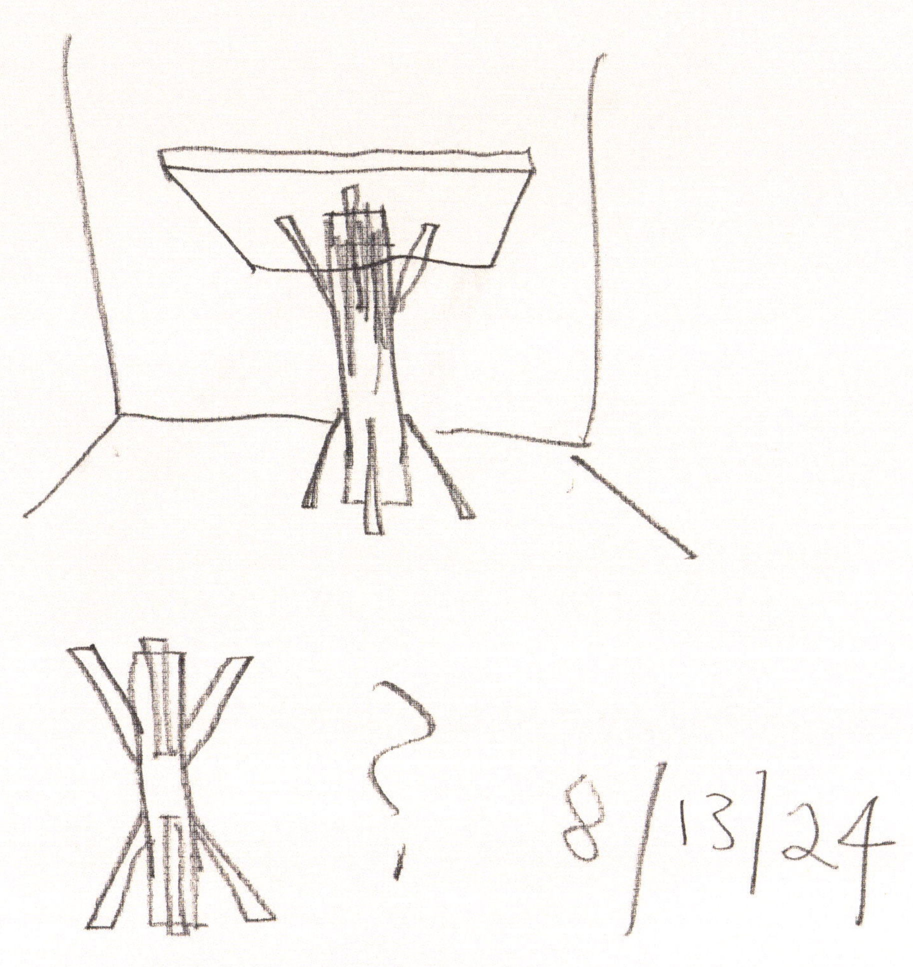
?
8/13/24

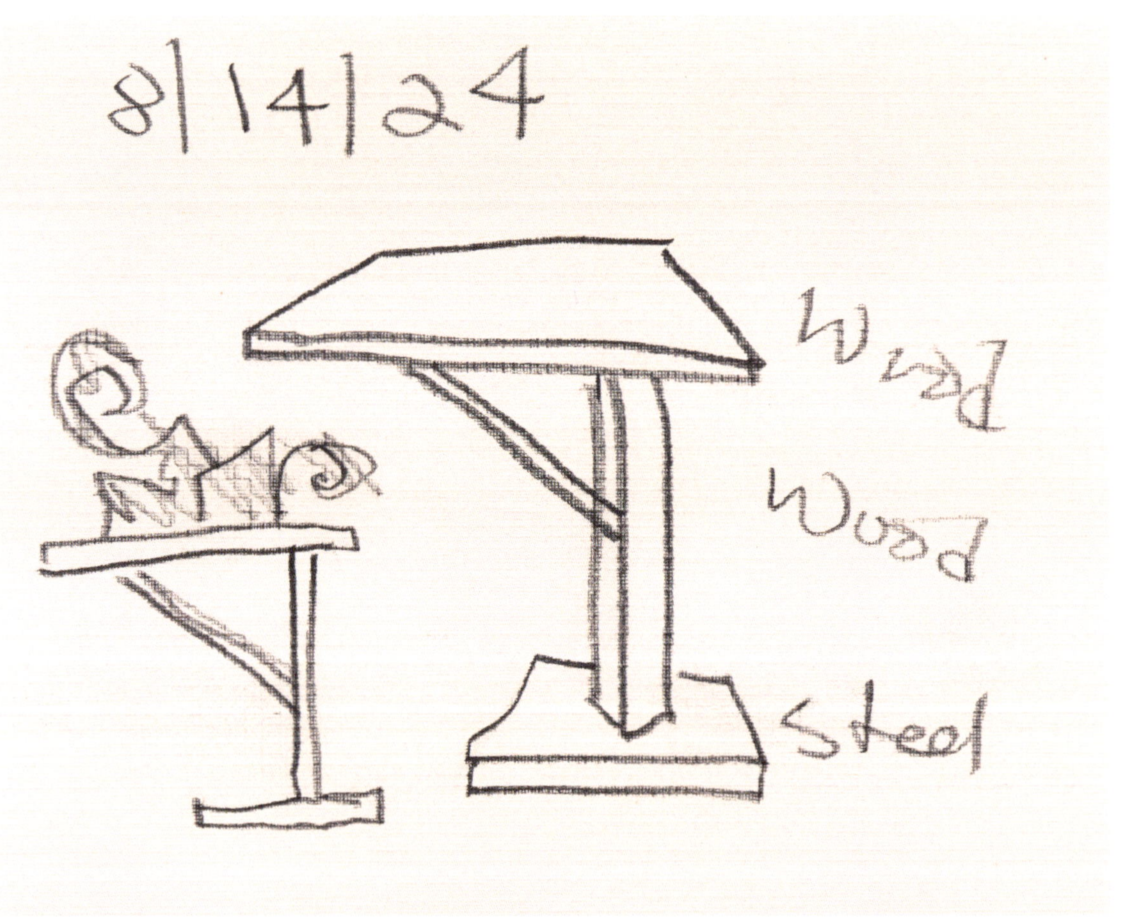

8/14/24
Warm
Wood
Steel

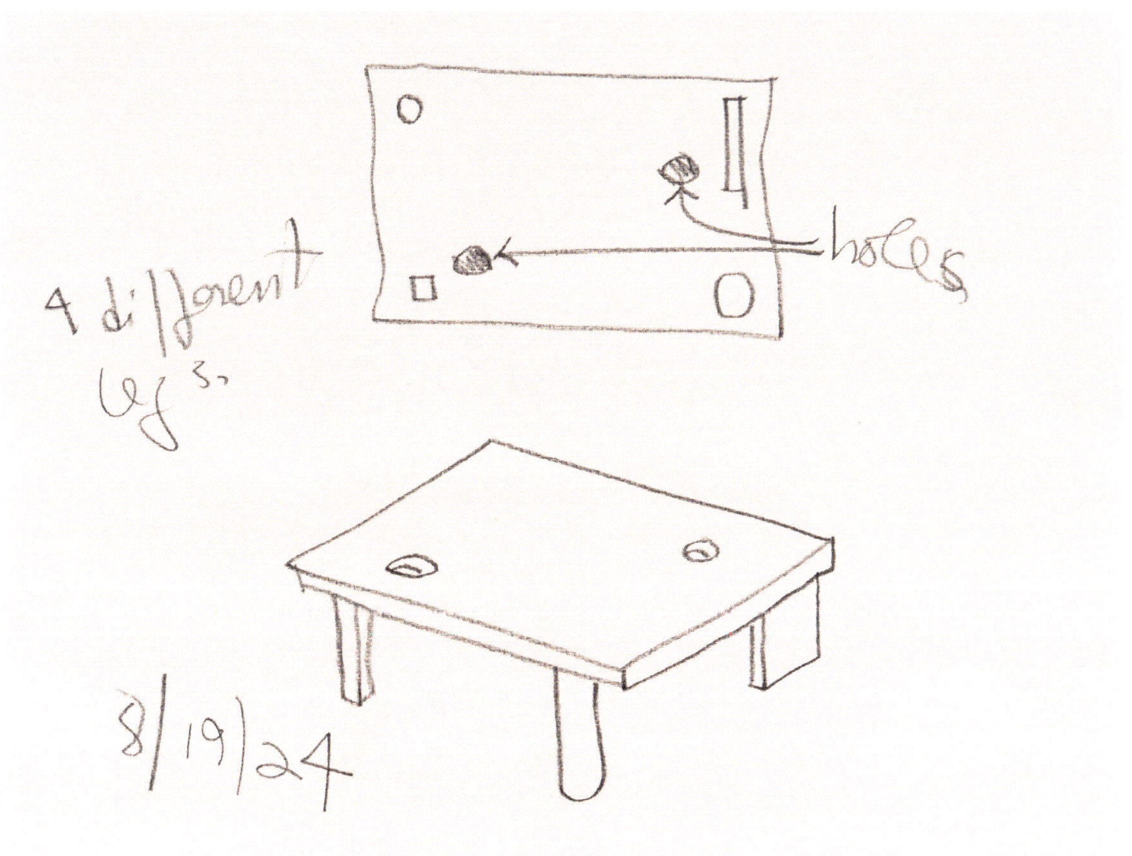
4 different
legs.

holes

8/19/24

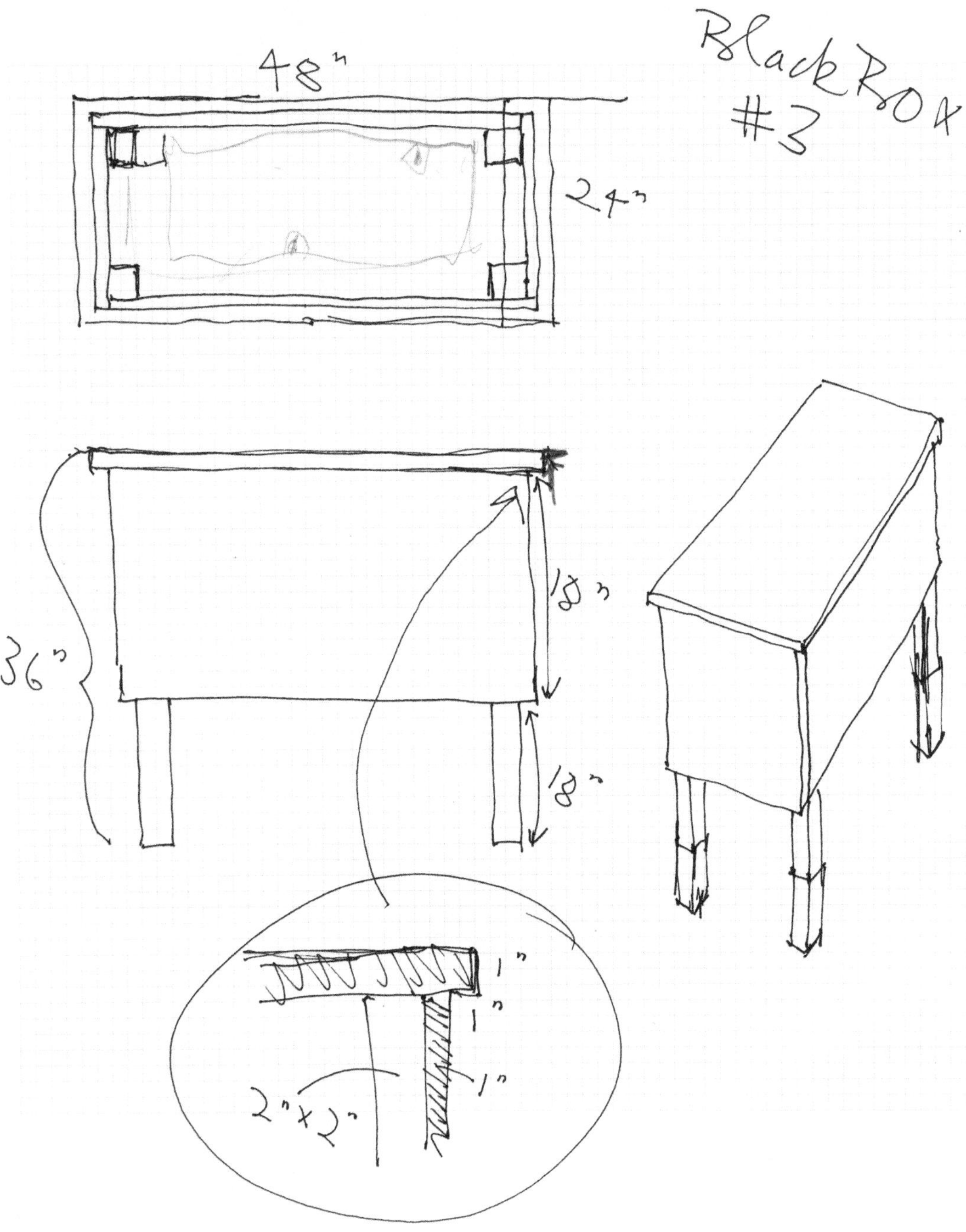
Black Box
#3
48"
24"
36"
18"
18"
2"x2"
1"
1"
1"

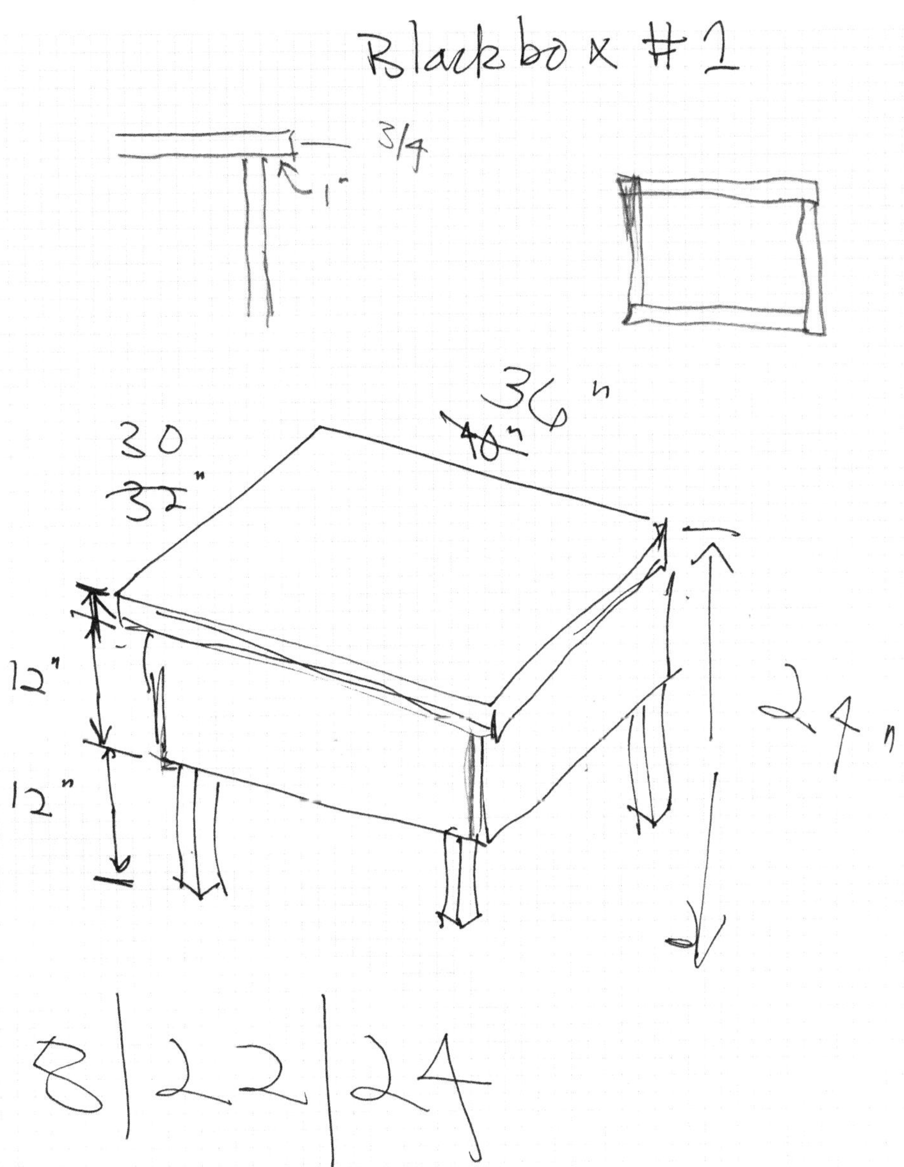

Blackbox #1
3/4
1"
36"
40"
30
32"
12"
12"
24"
8/22/24

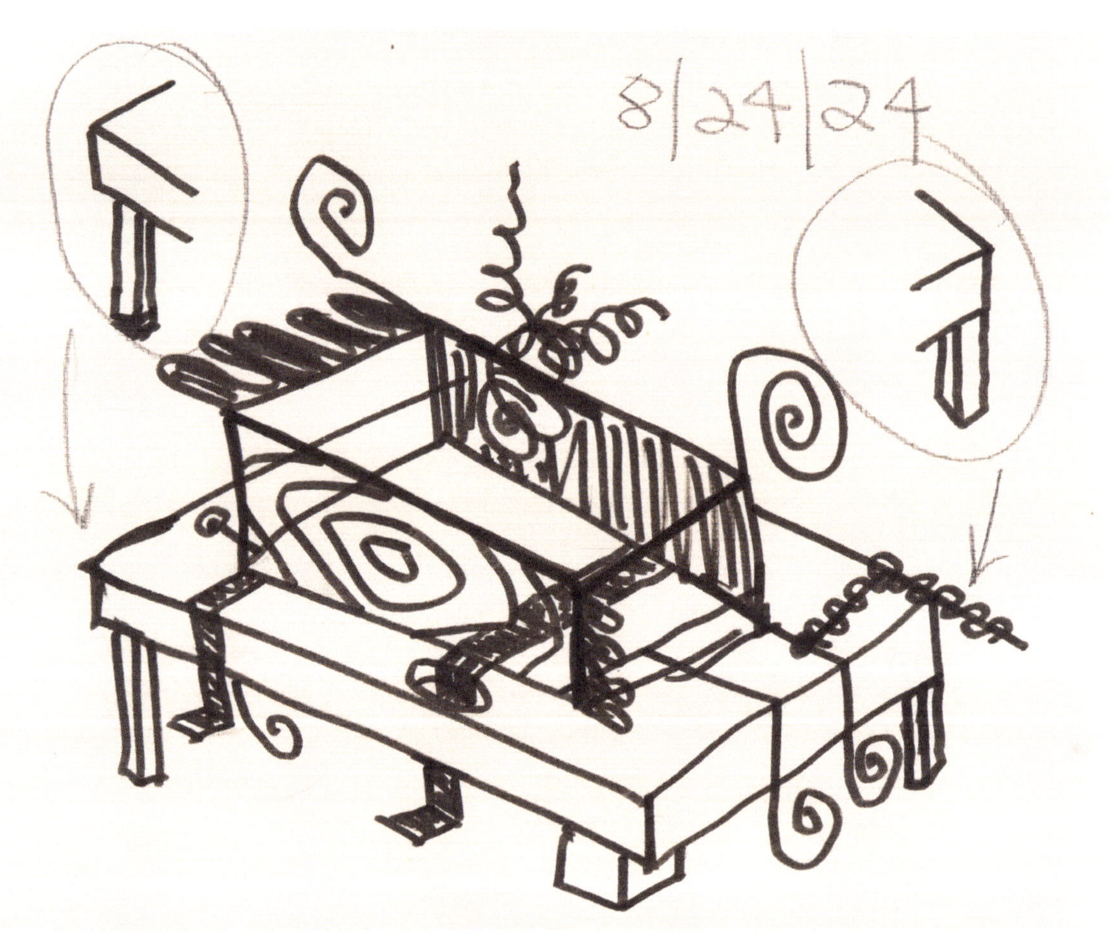

8/24/24

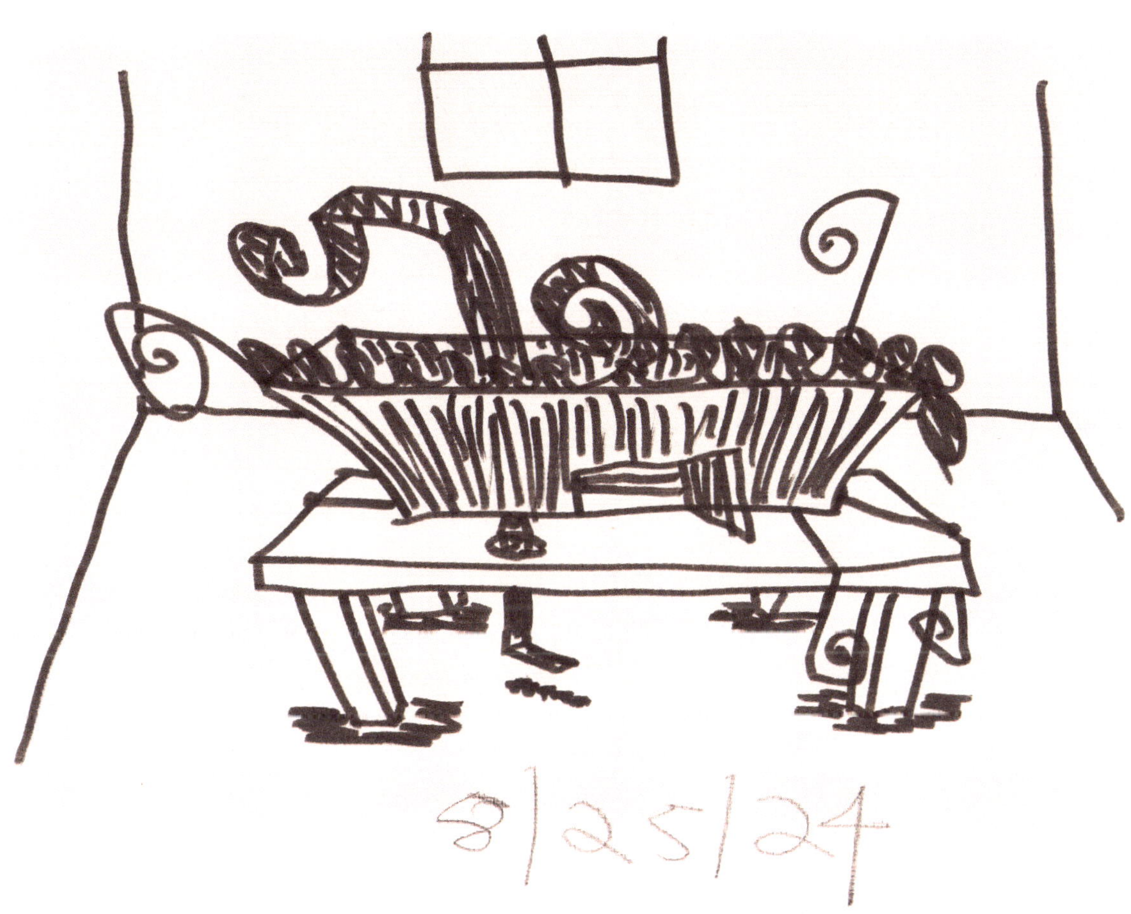

8/25/24

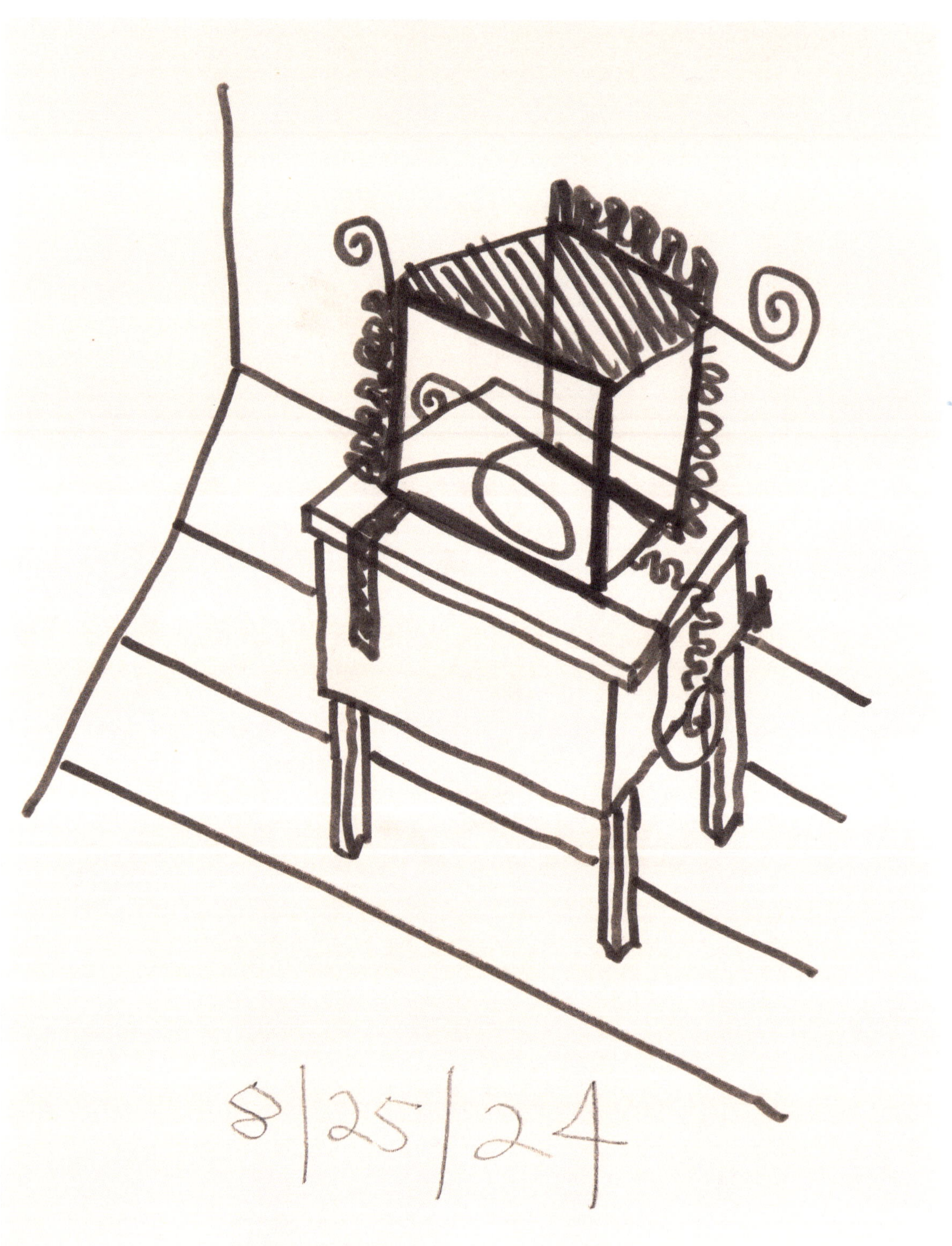

8/25/24

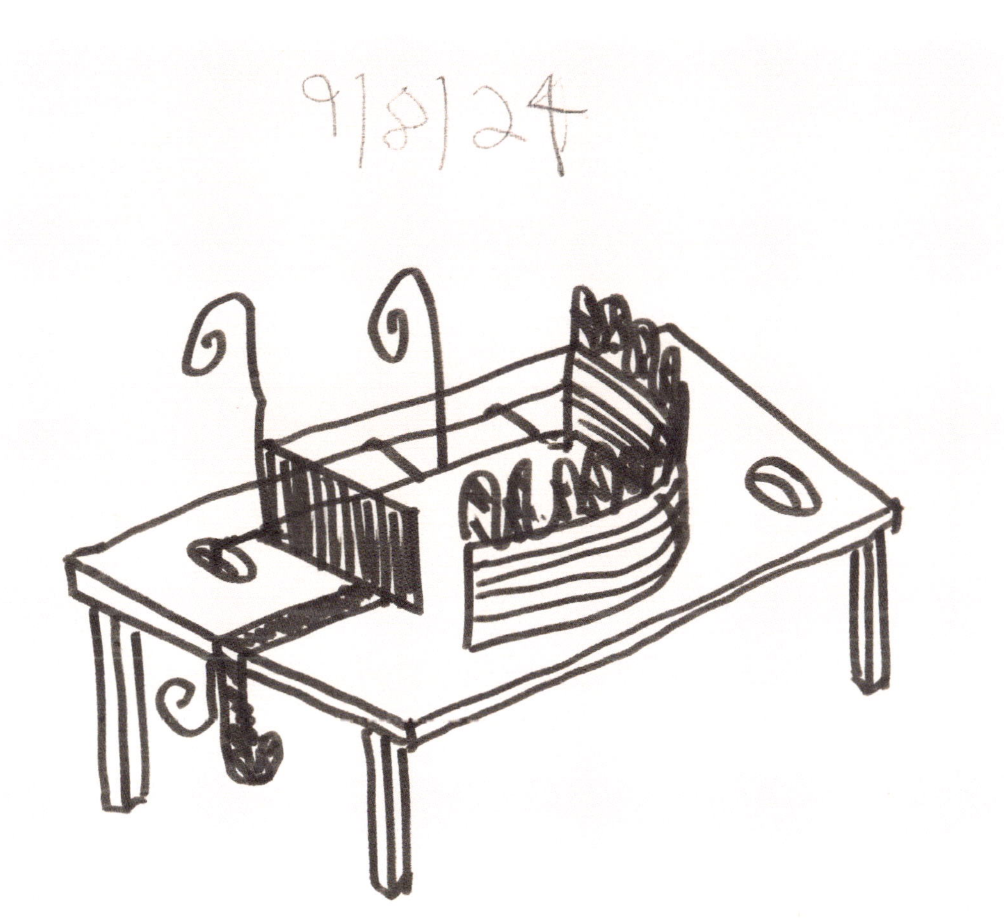

9/8/24

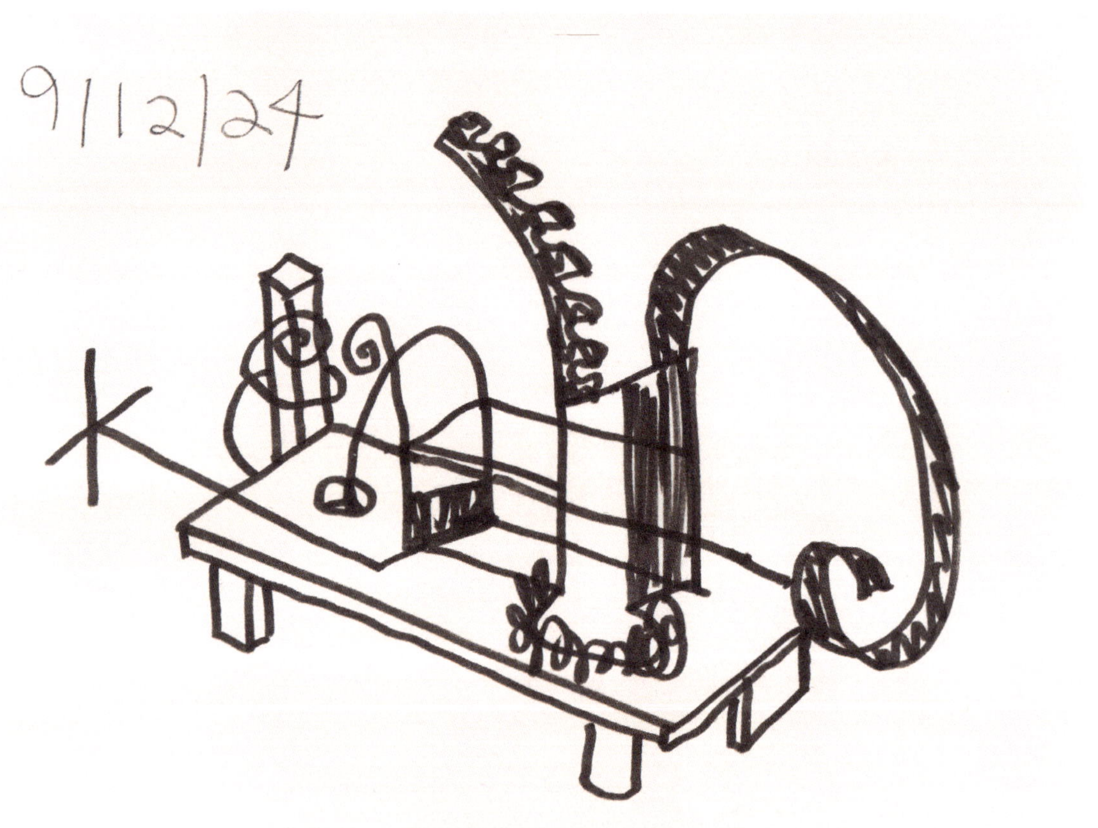

9/12/24

9/14/24

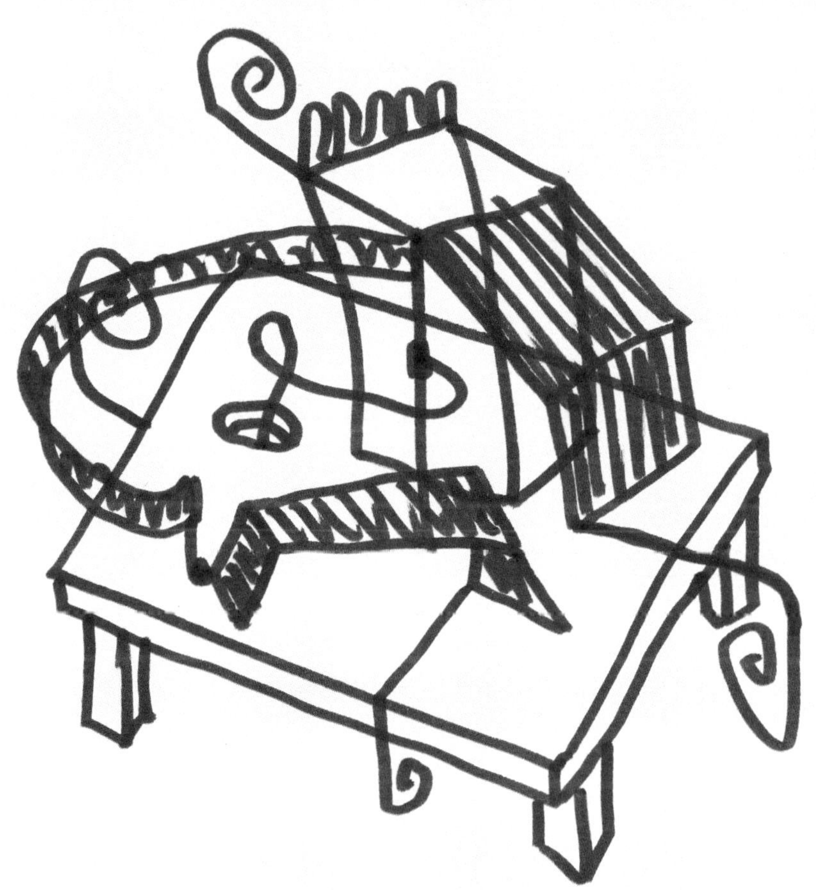

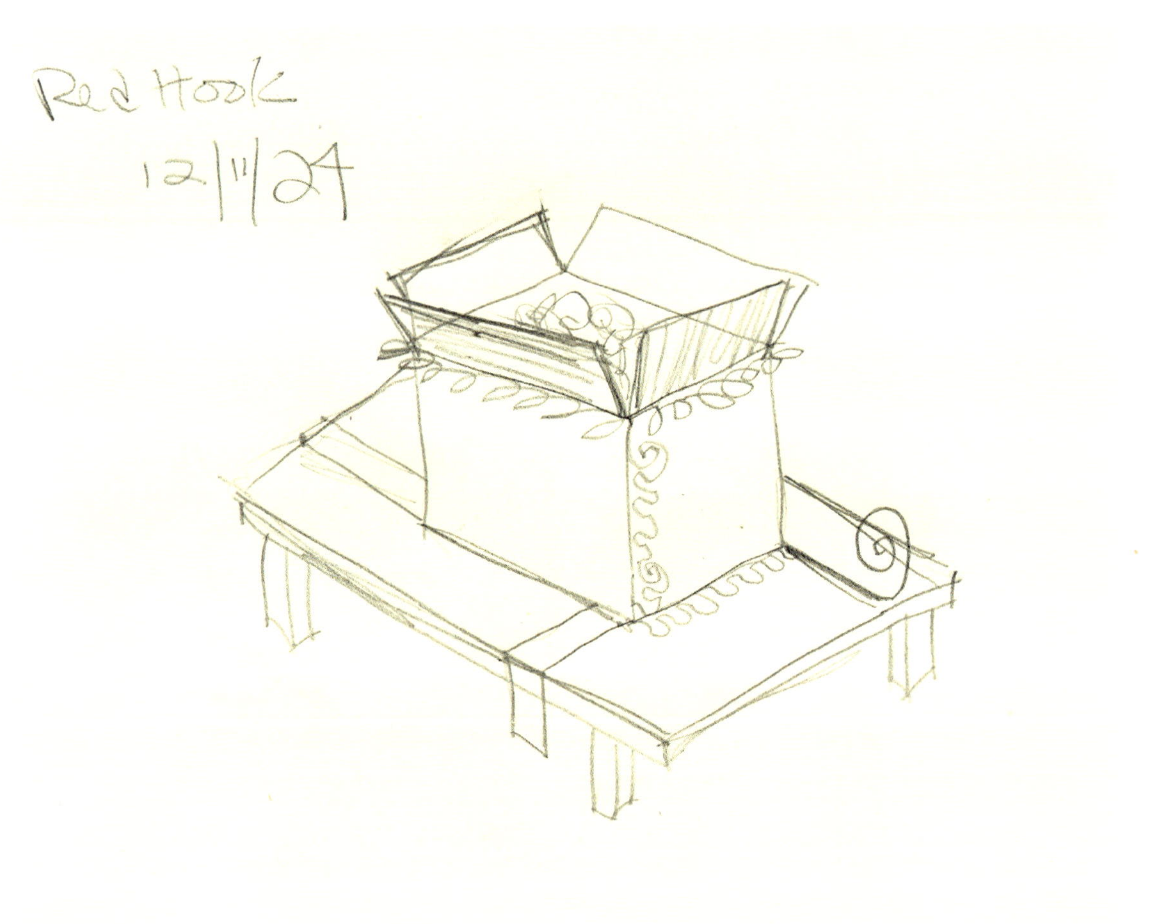
Red Hook
12/11/27

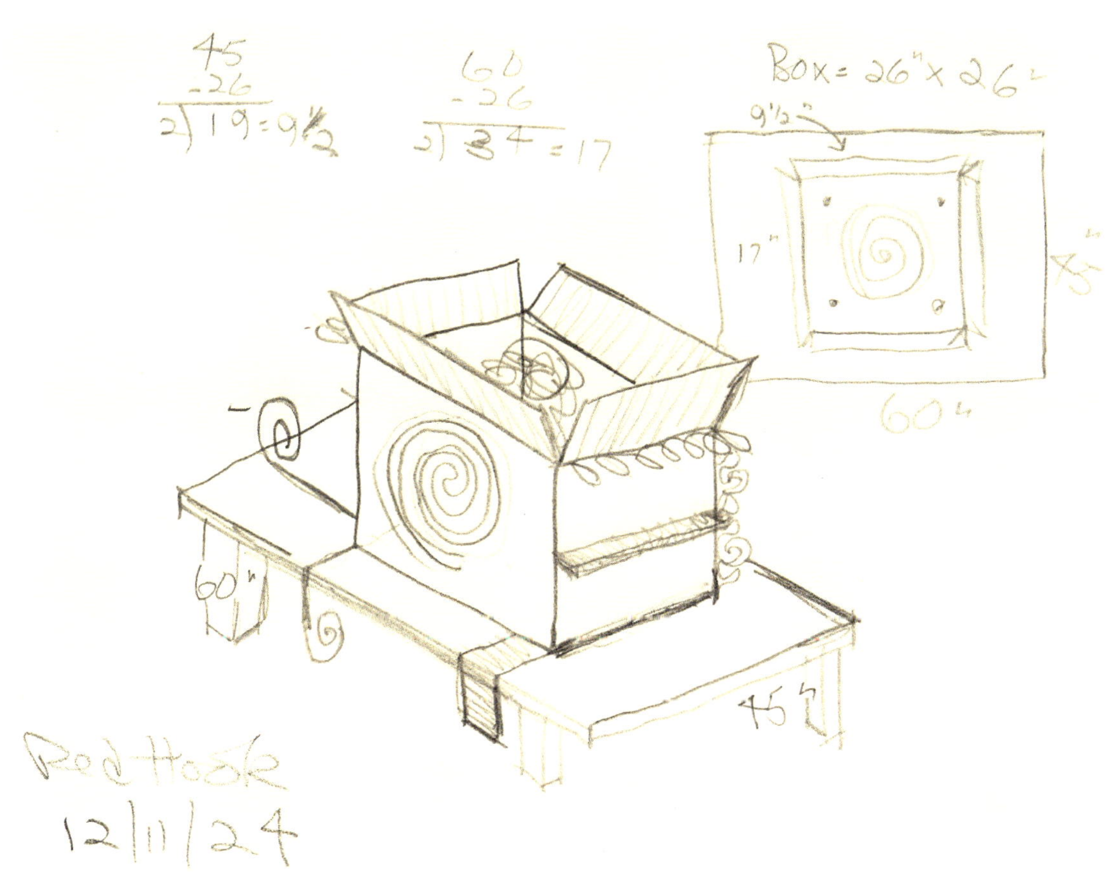
45
-26
2)19 = 9½
60
-26
2)34 = 17
Box = 26" x 26"
9½"
17"
60"
60"
45"
Red Hook
12/11/24

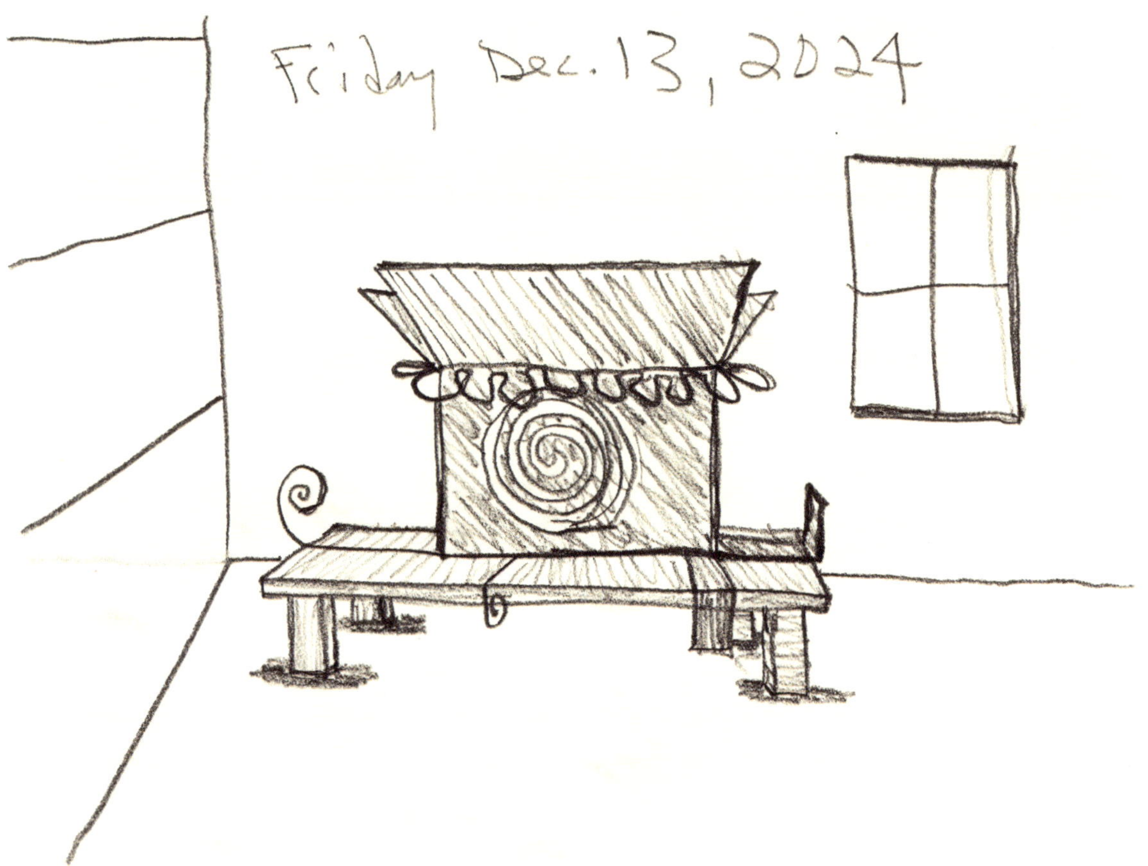

Friday Dec. 13, 2024

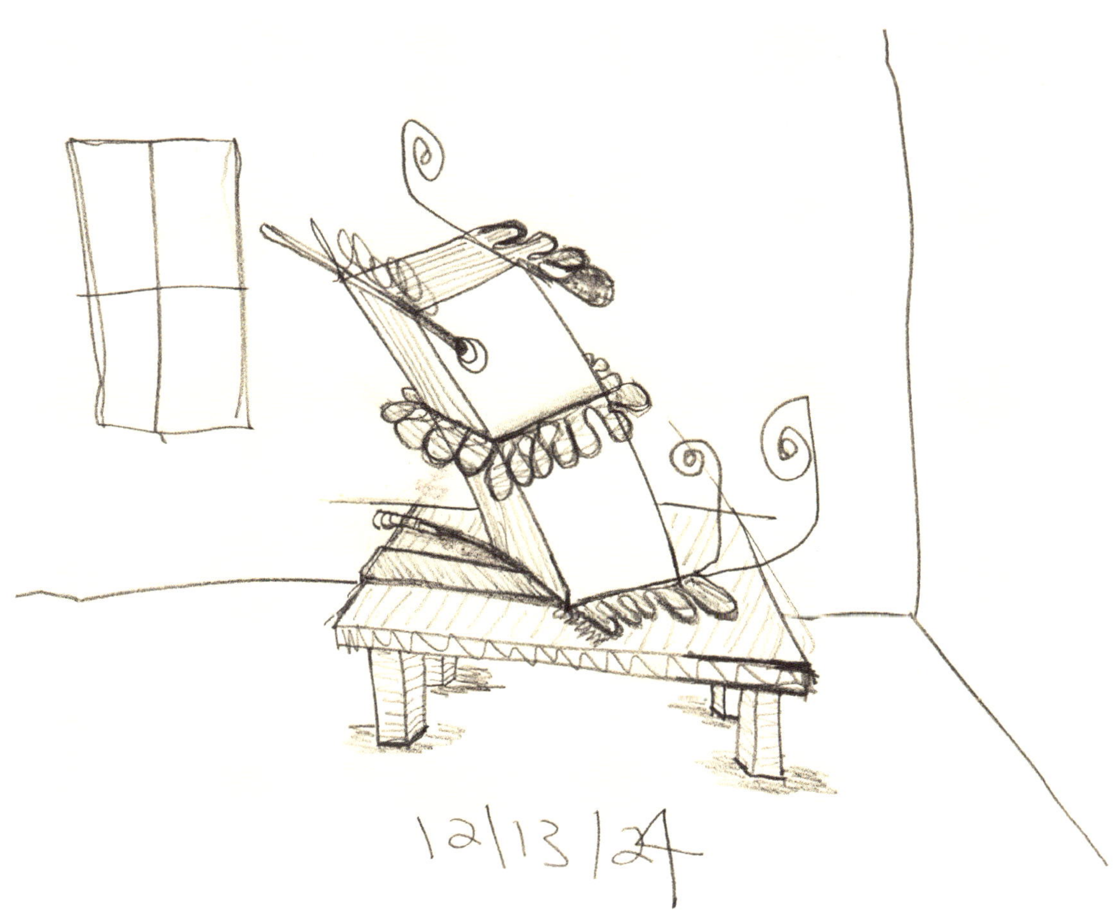
12/13/24

Stainless steel

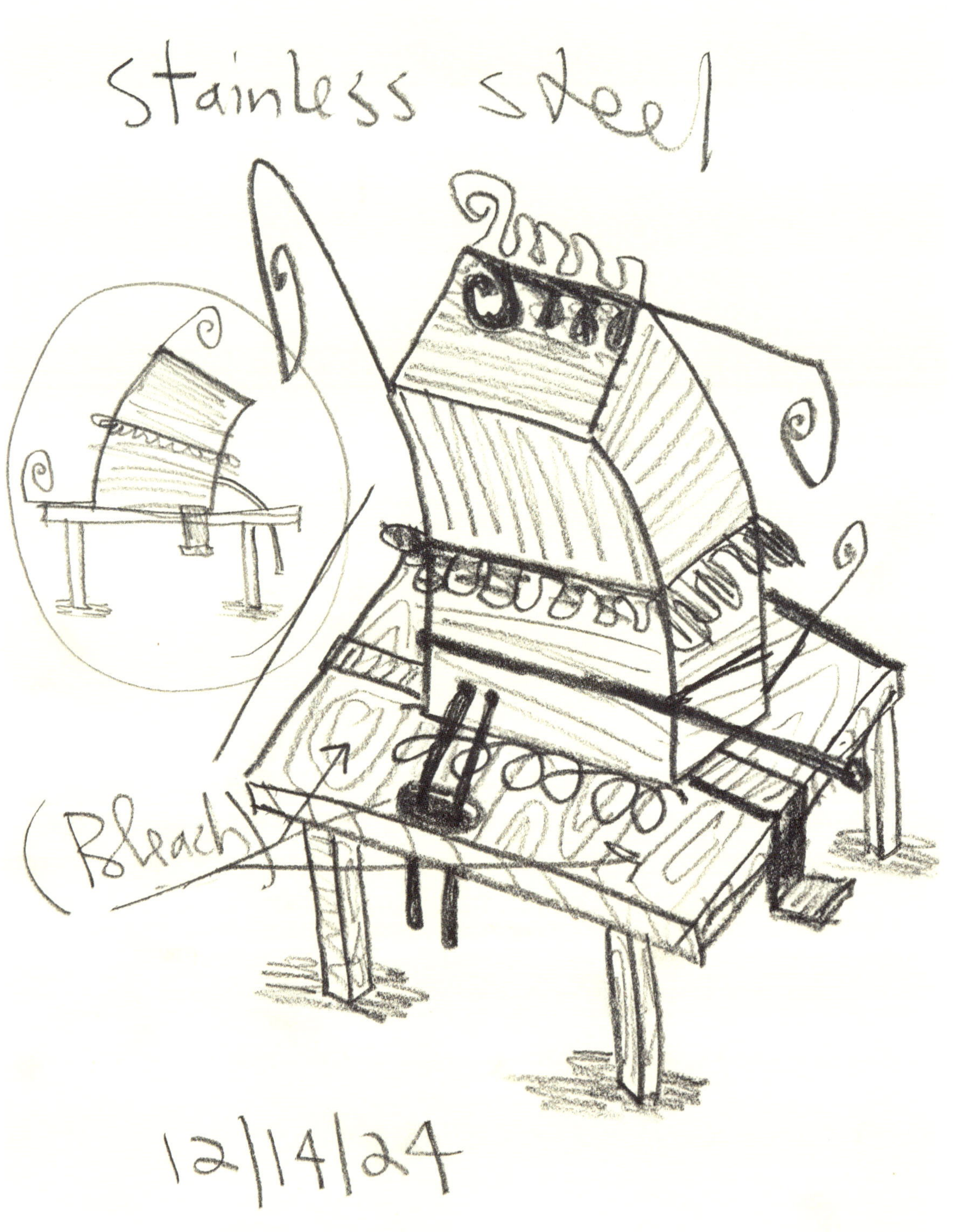

12/14/24

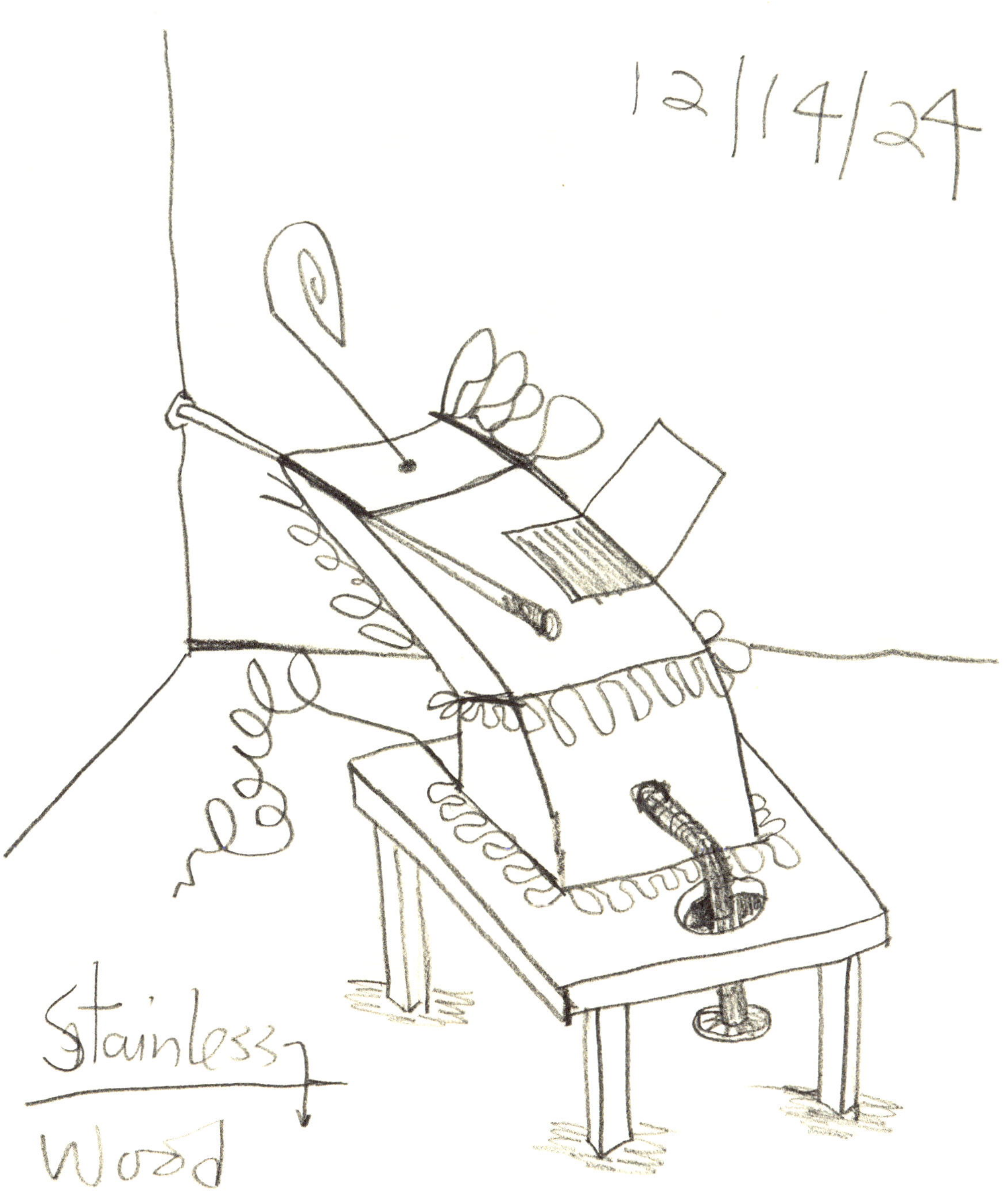

12/14/24
Stainless
Wood

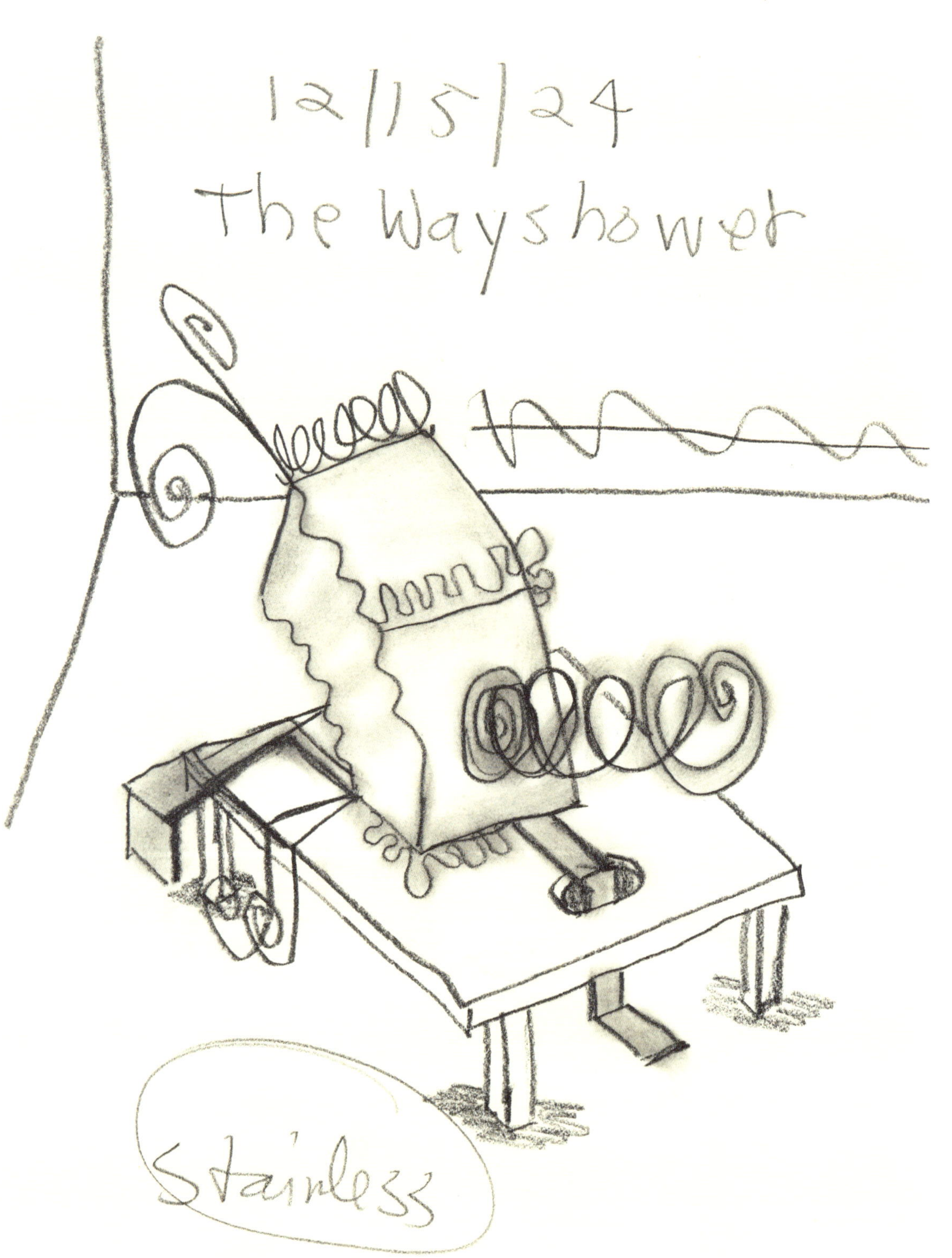

12/15/24
The Wayshower
Stainless

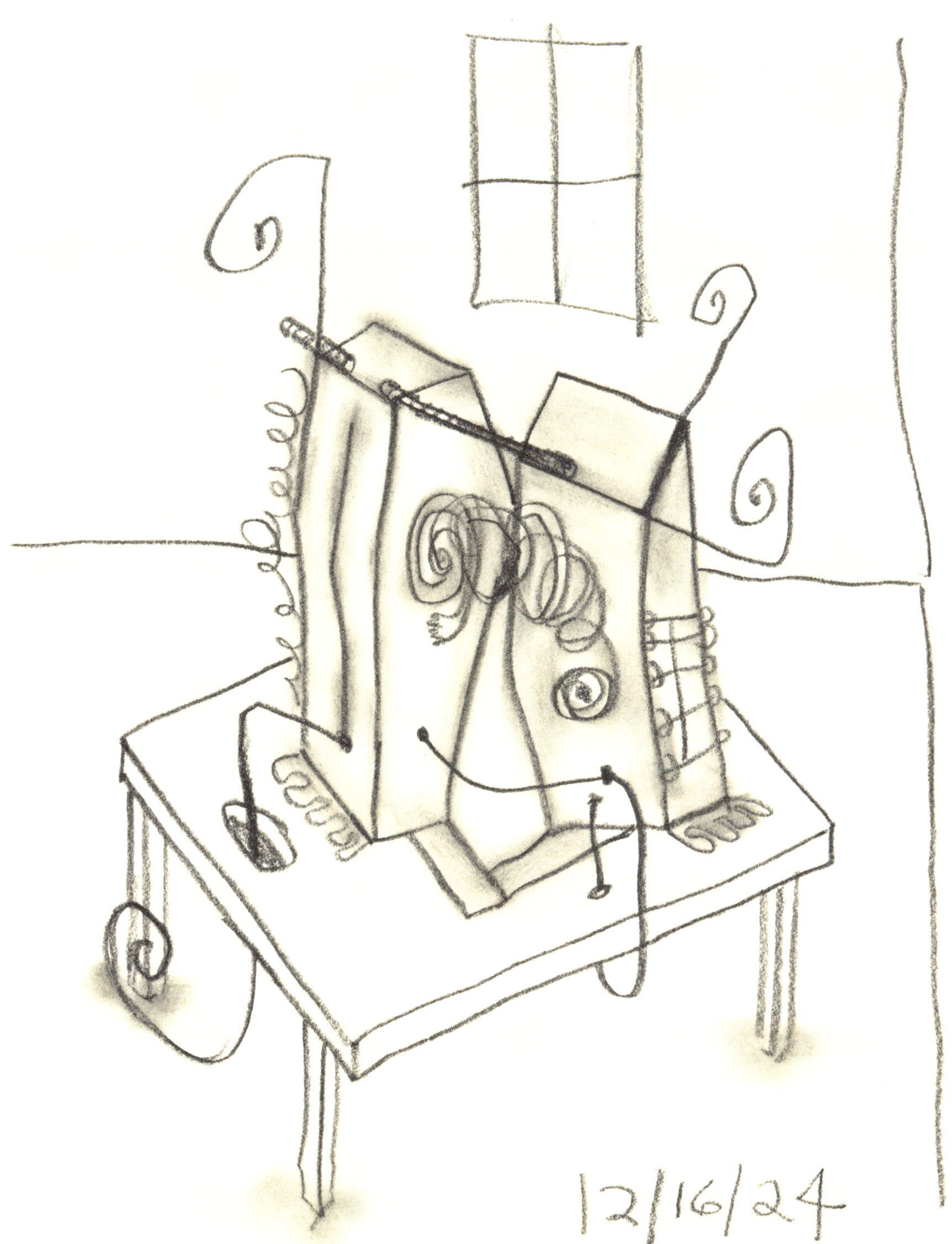

12/16/24

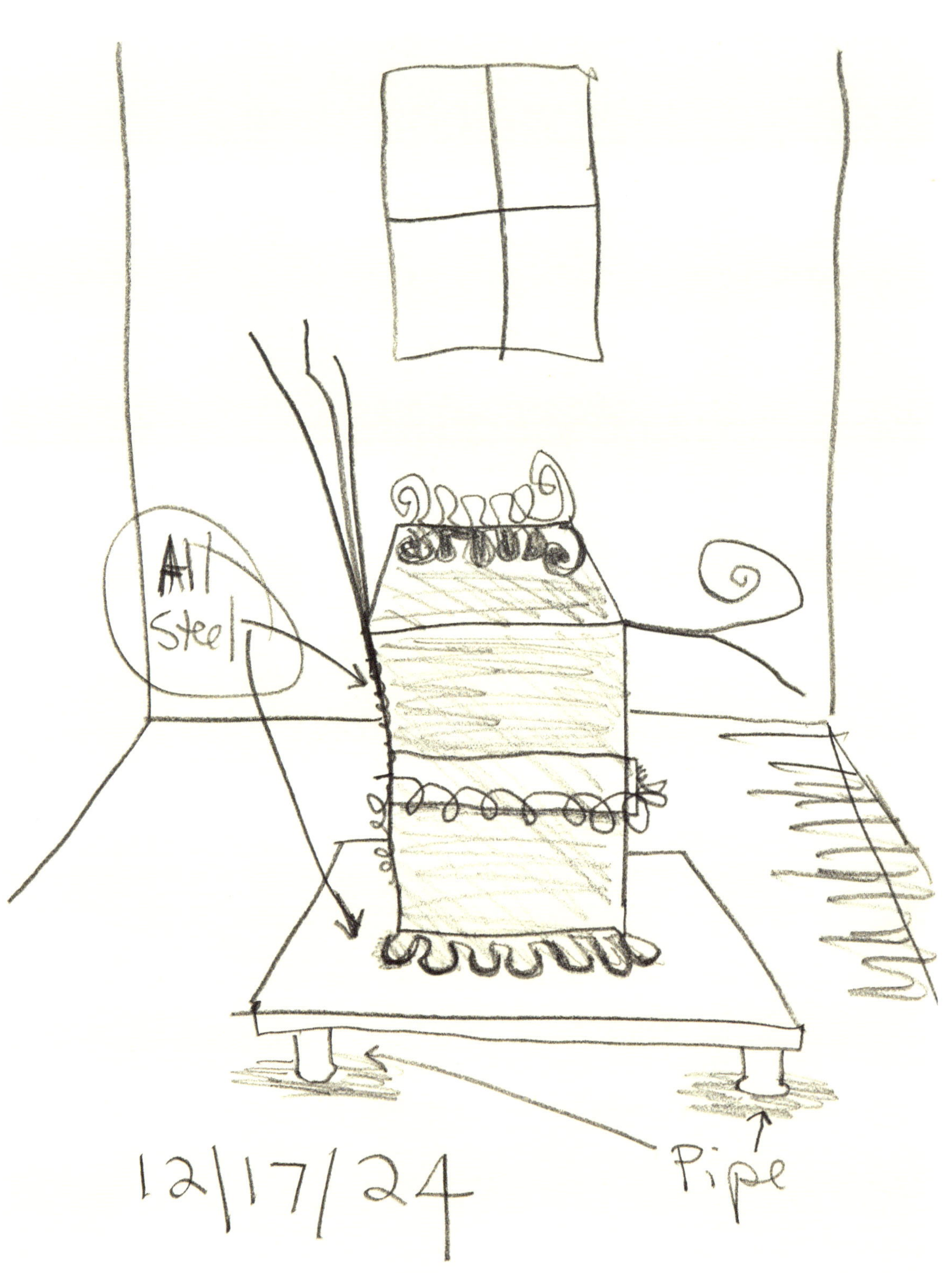

All
Steel
Pipe
12/17/24

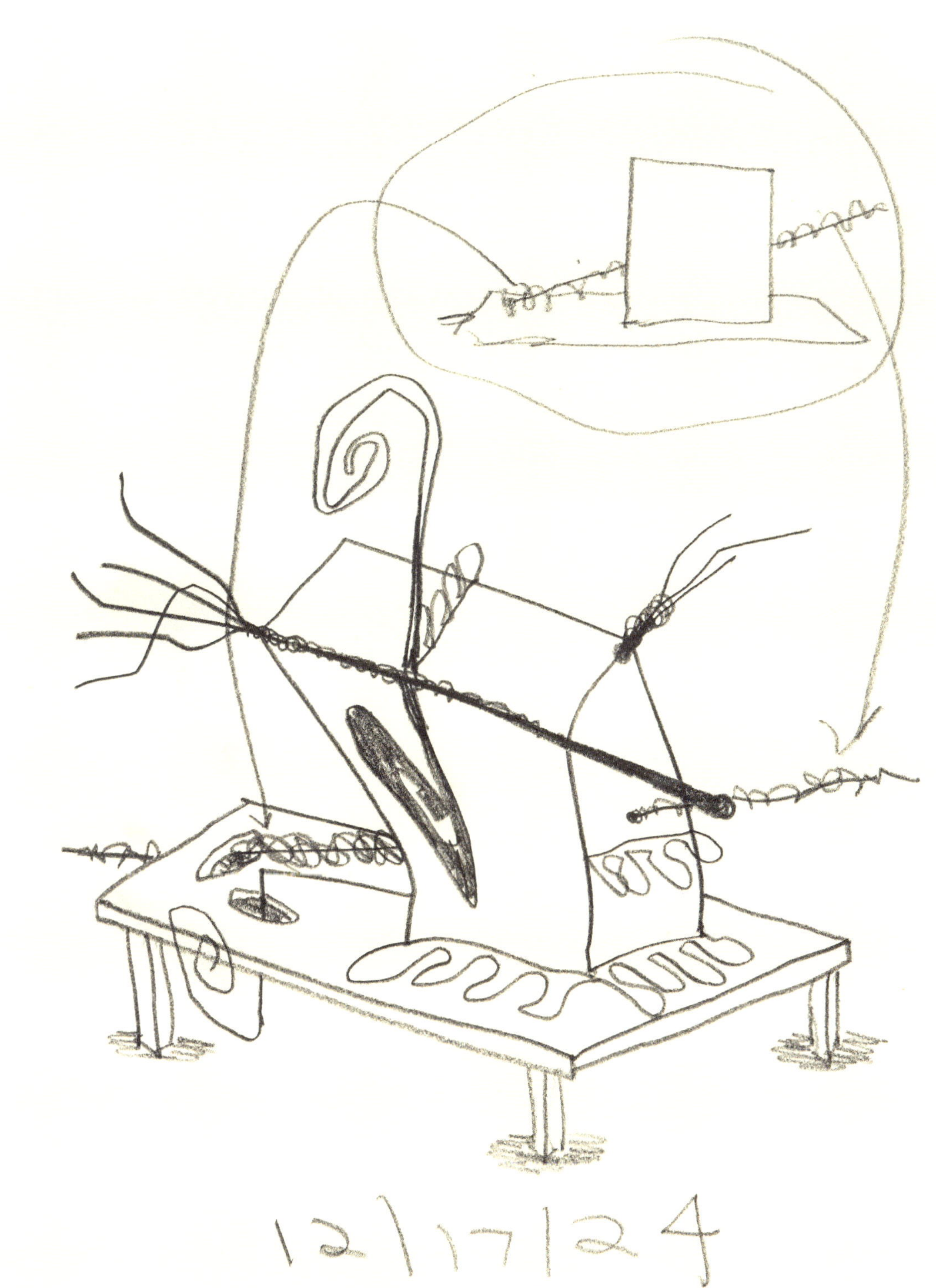

12/17/24

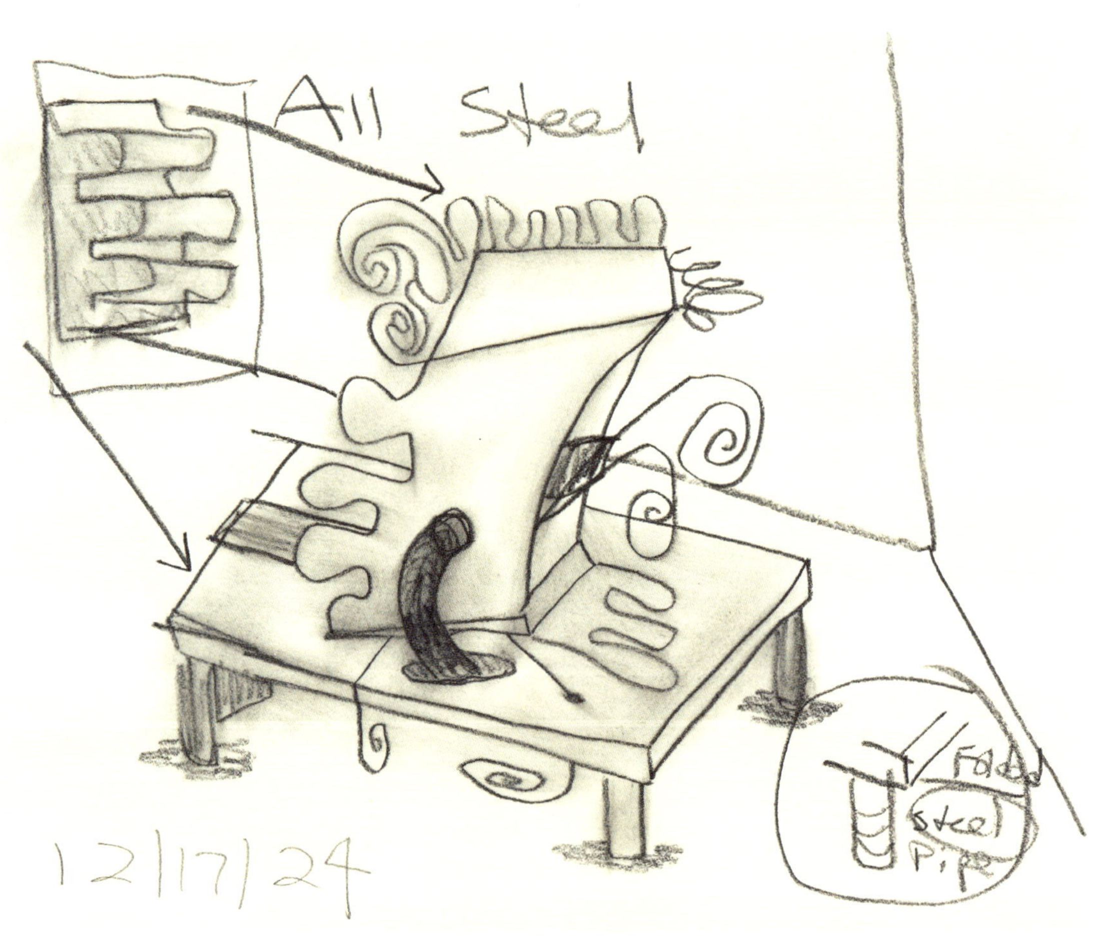
All Steel
12/17/24
Fold
Steel
Pipe

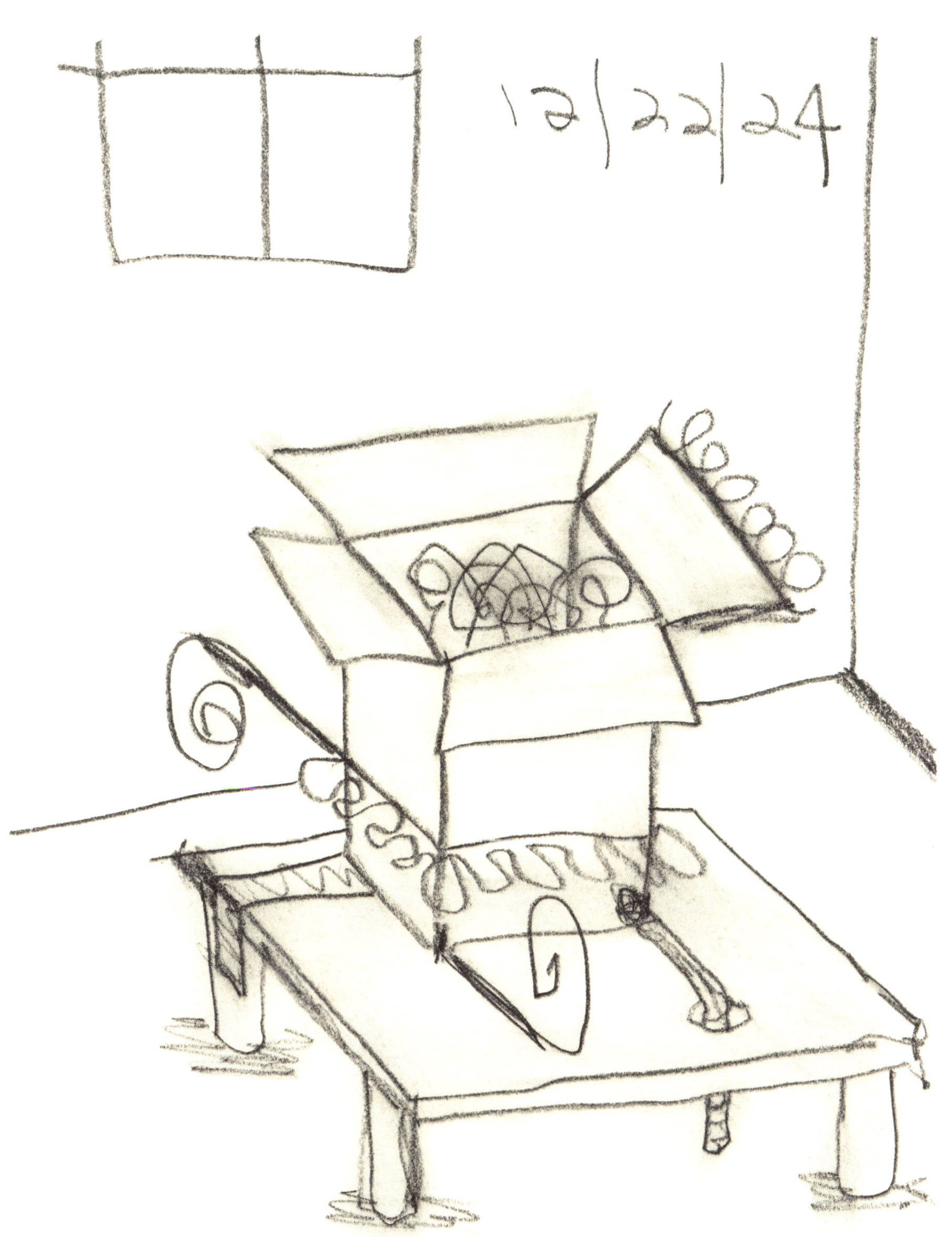

12/22/24

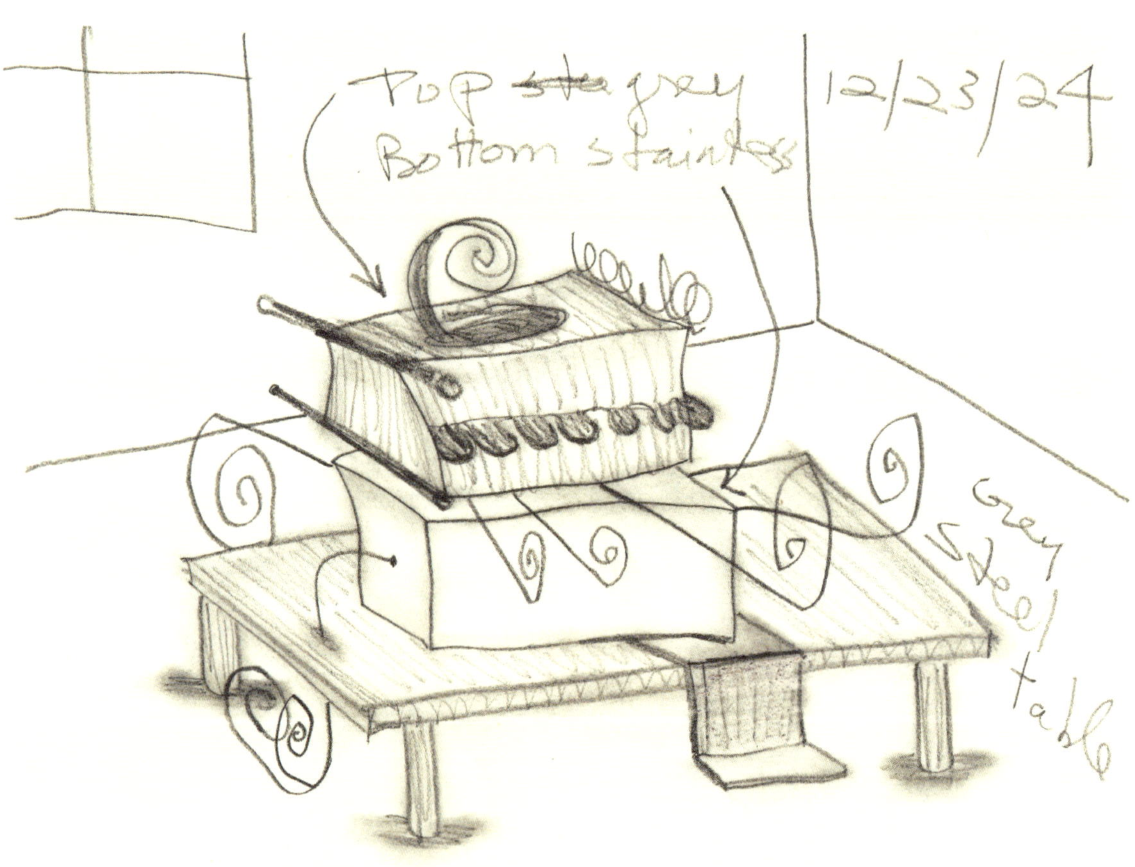
Pop ~~the~~ grey
Bottom stainless
12/23/24
Grey
Steel
table

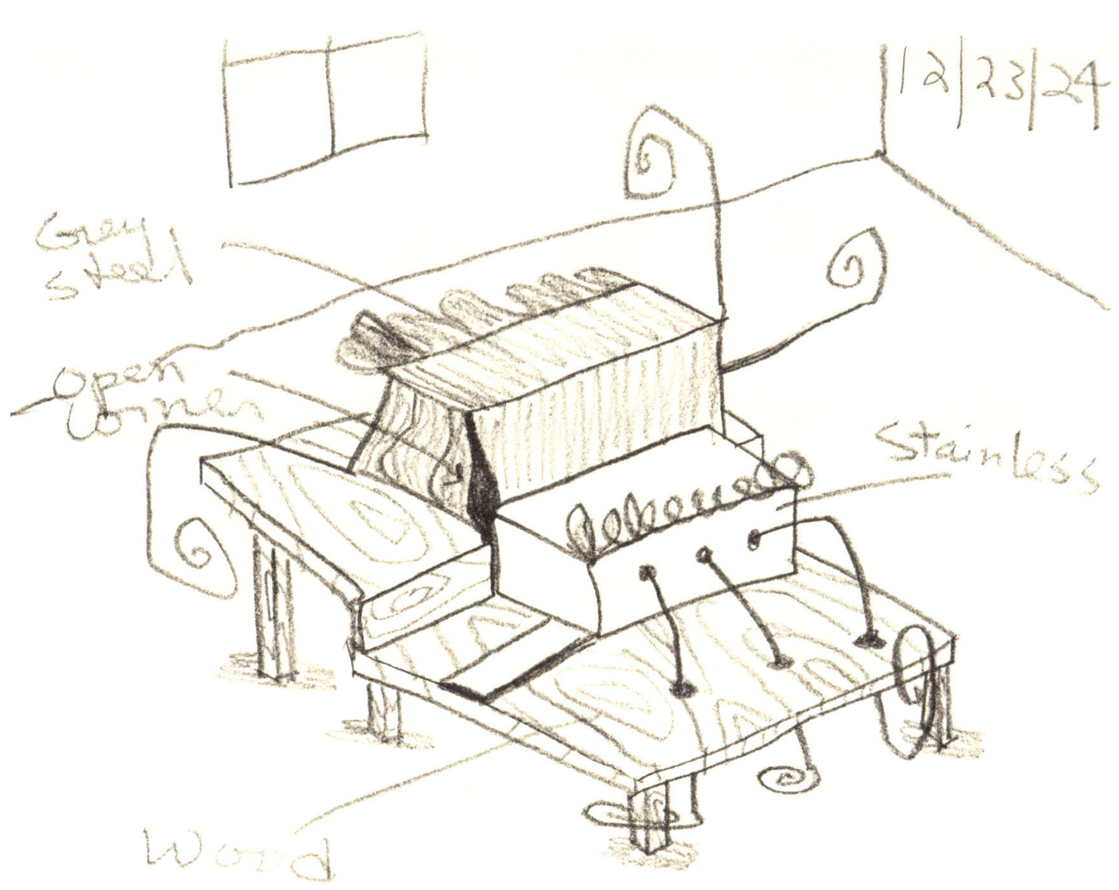
Grey
Steel
Open
Corner
Stainless
Wood
12/23/24

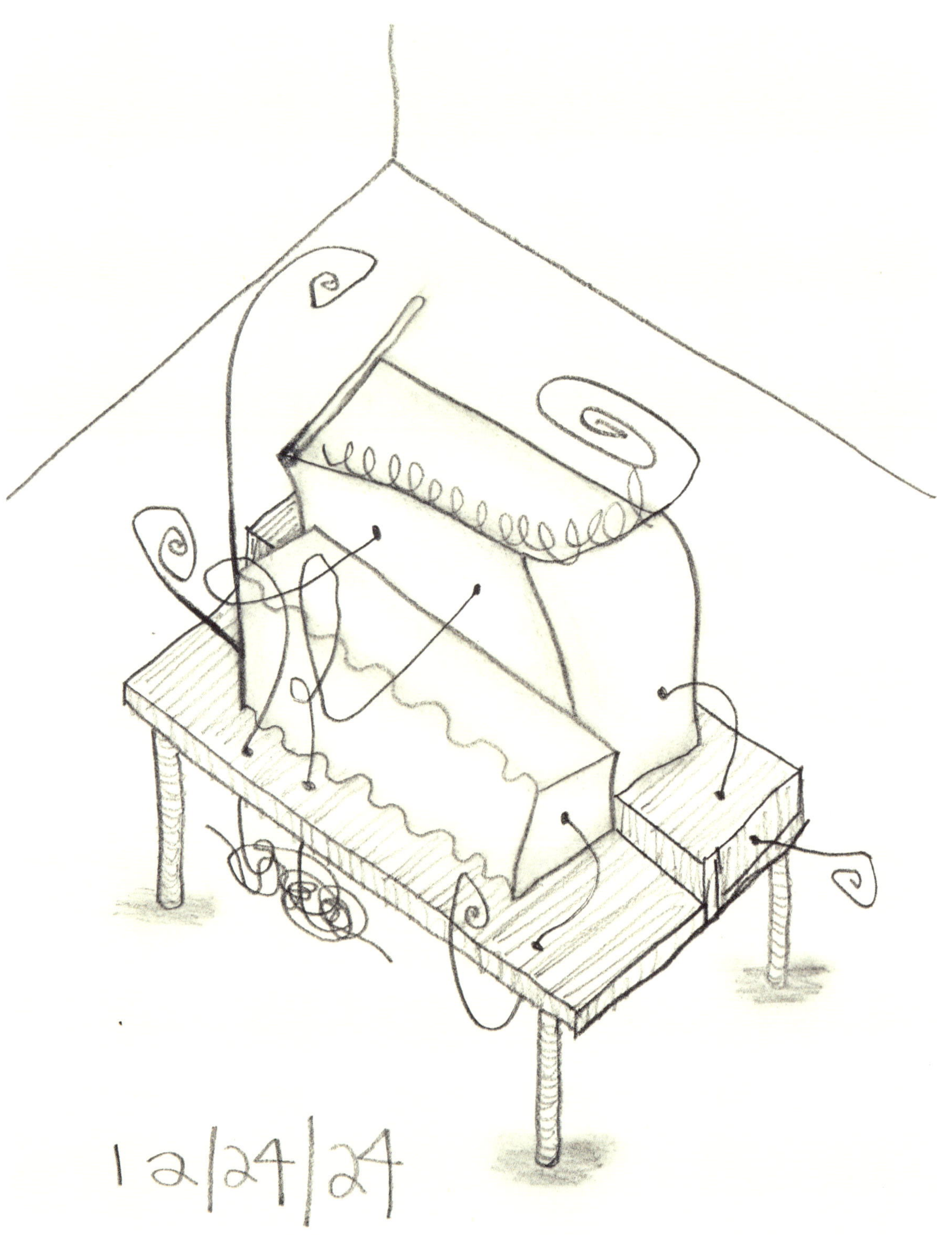

12/24/24

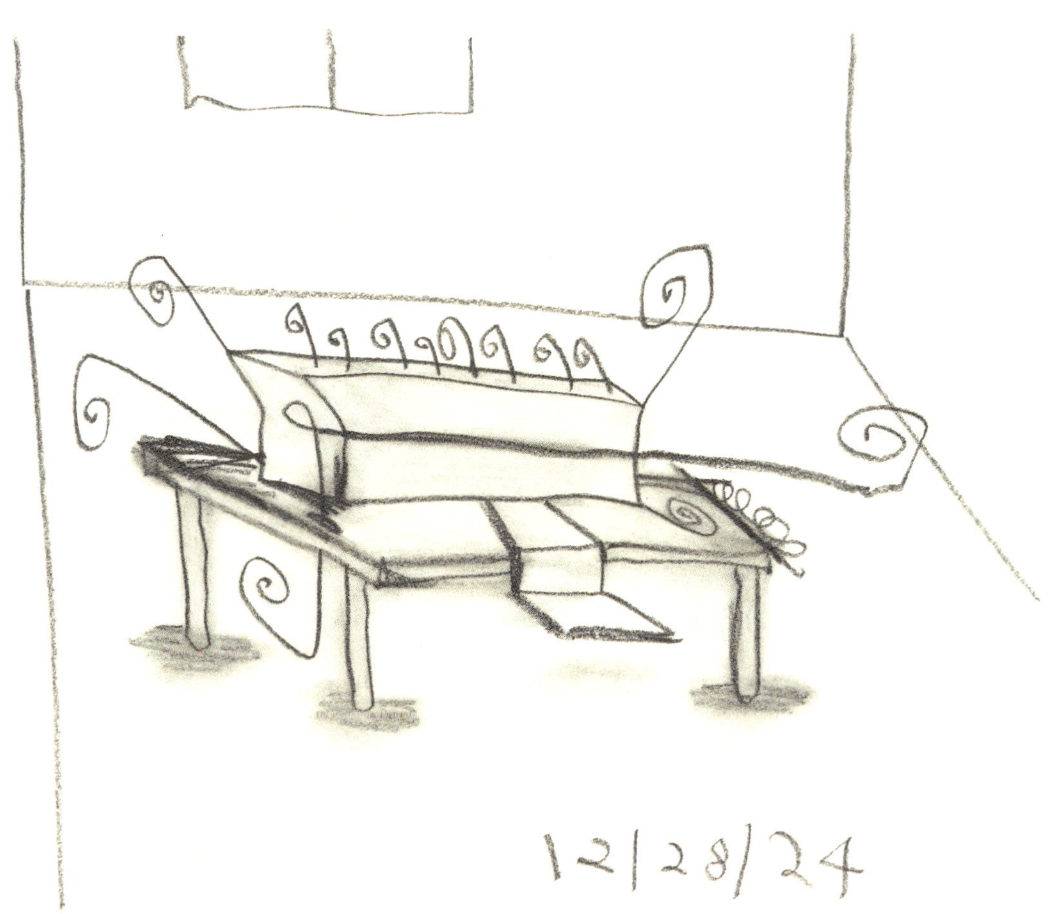

12/28/24

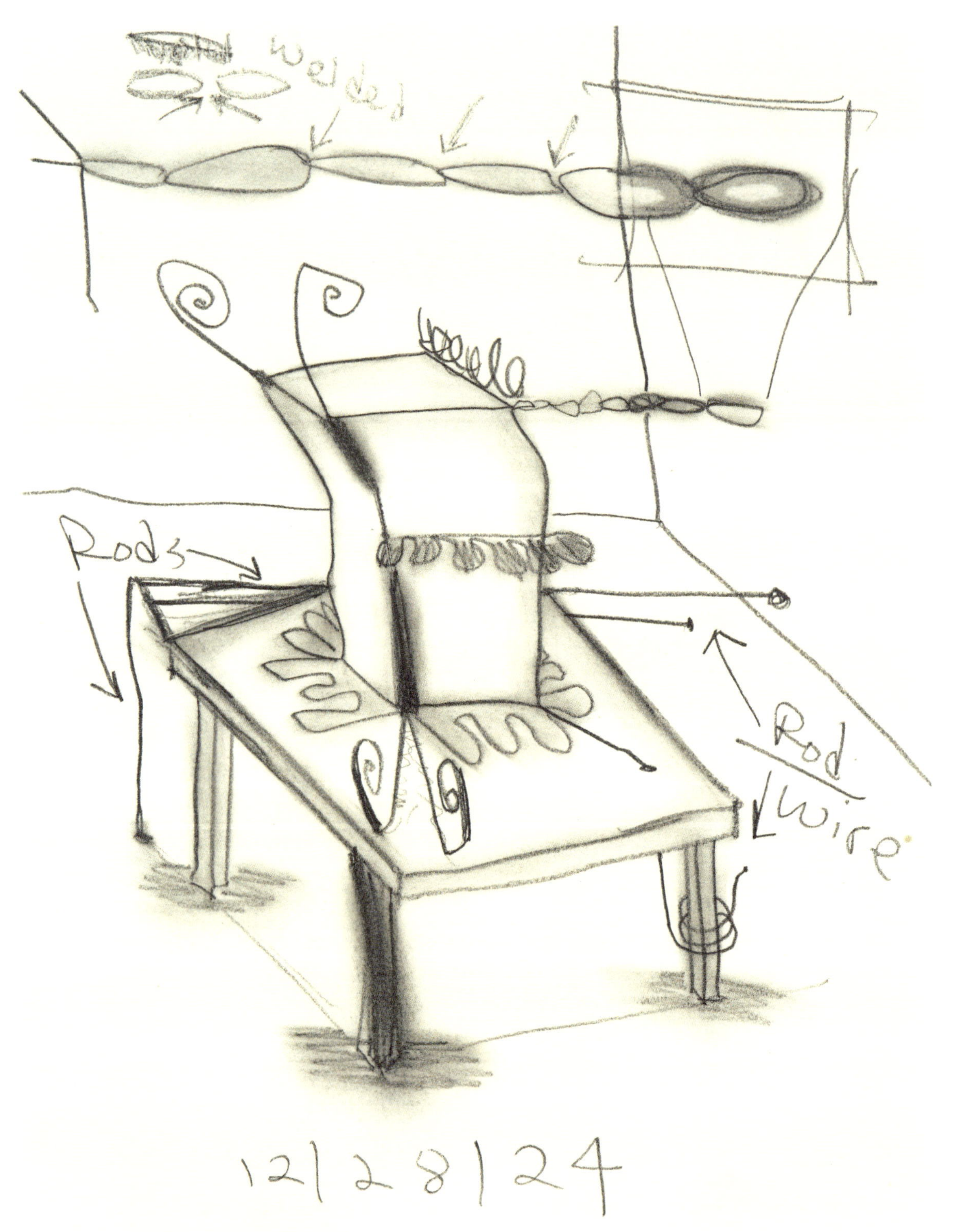
Welded
Rods
Rod
Wire
12/28/24

A sculpture of a
sculpture on a table

12/28/24

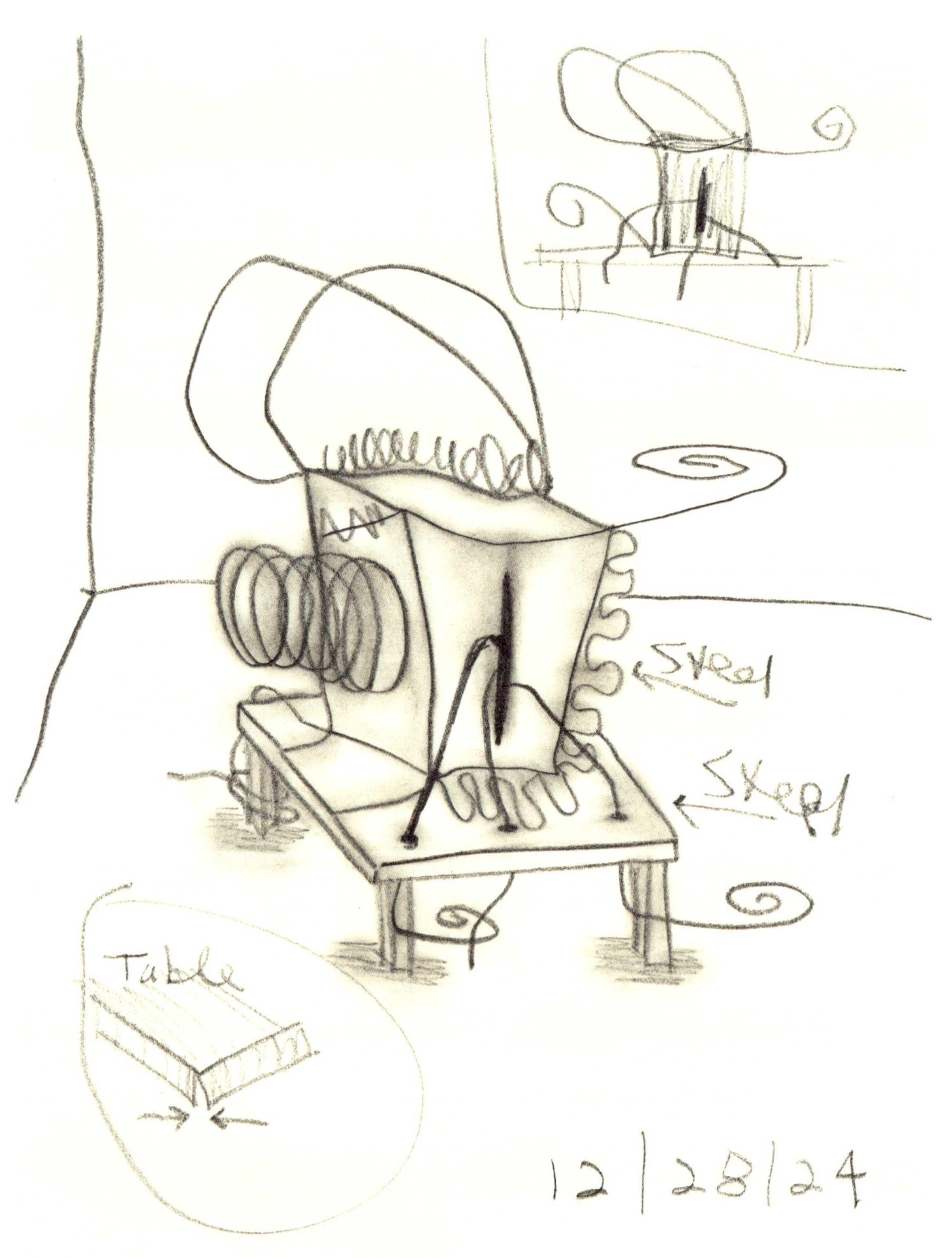

Svrel
Skepl
Table
12/28/24

12/29/24

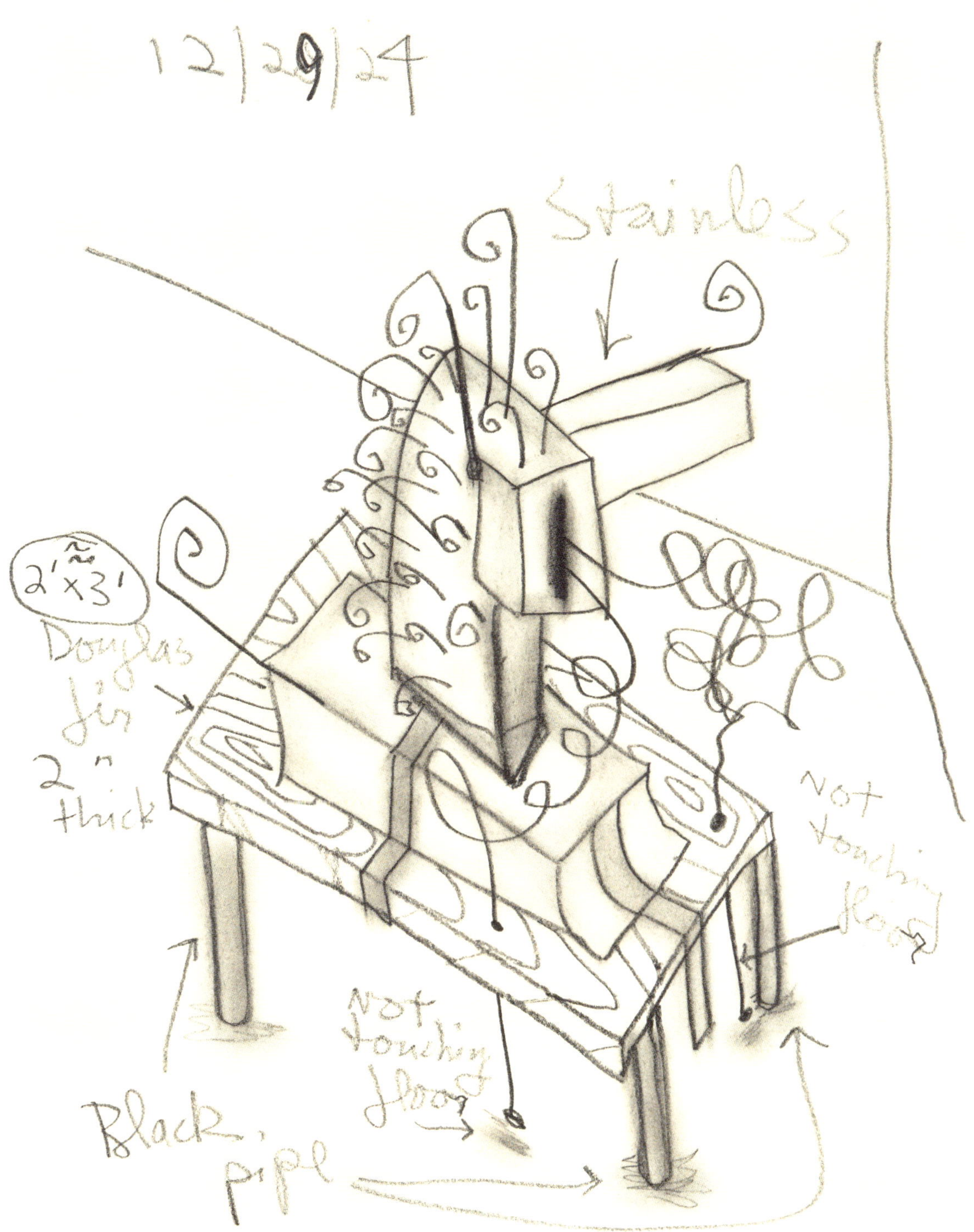

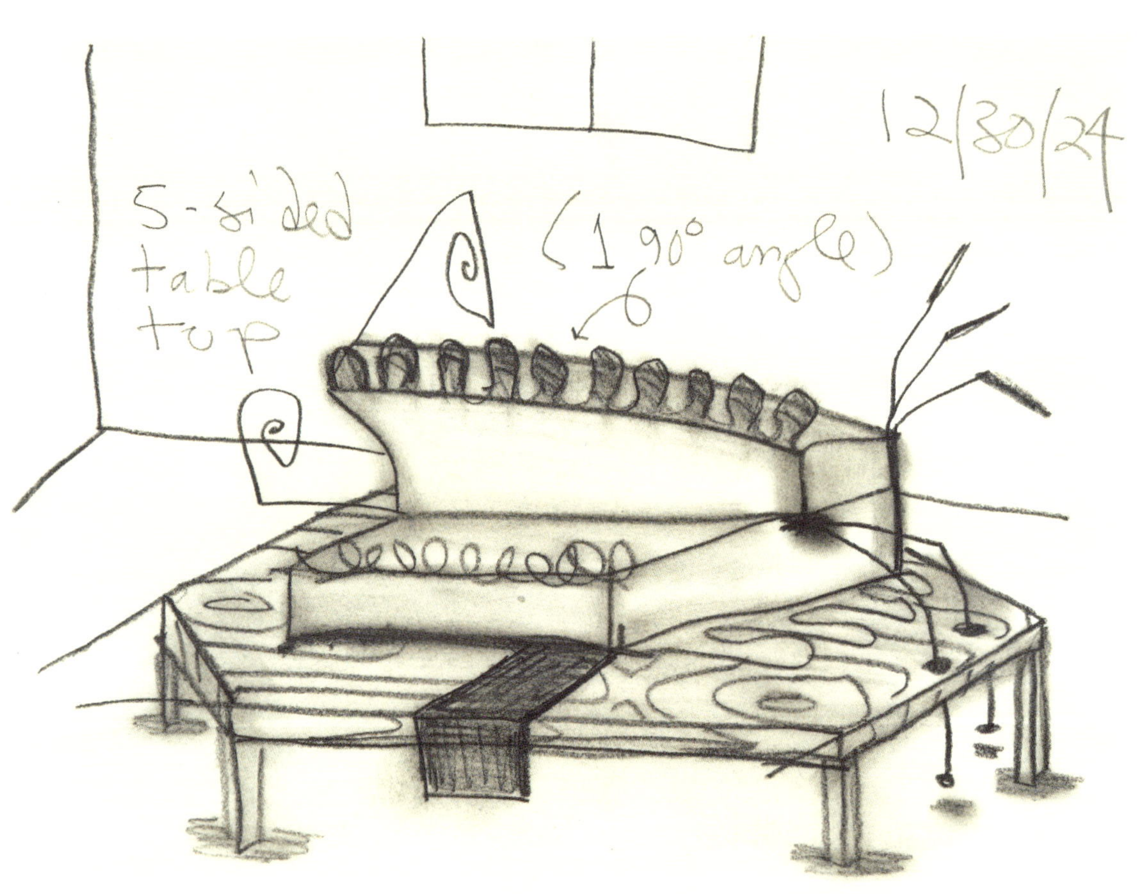

12/30/24
5-sided table top
(∠190° angle)

12/30/24

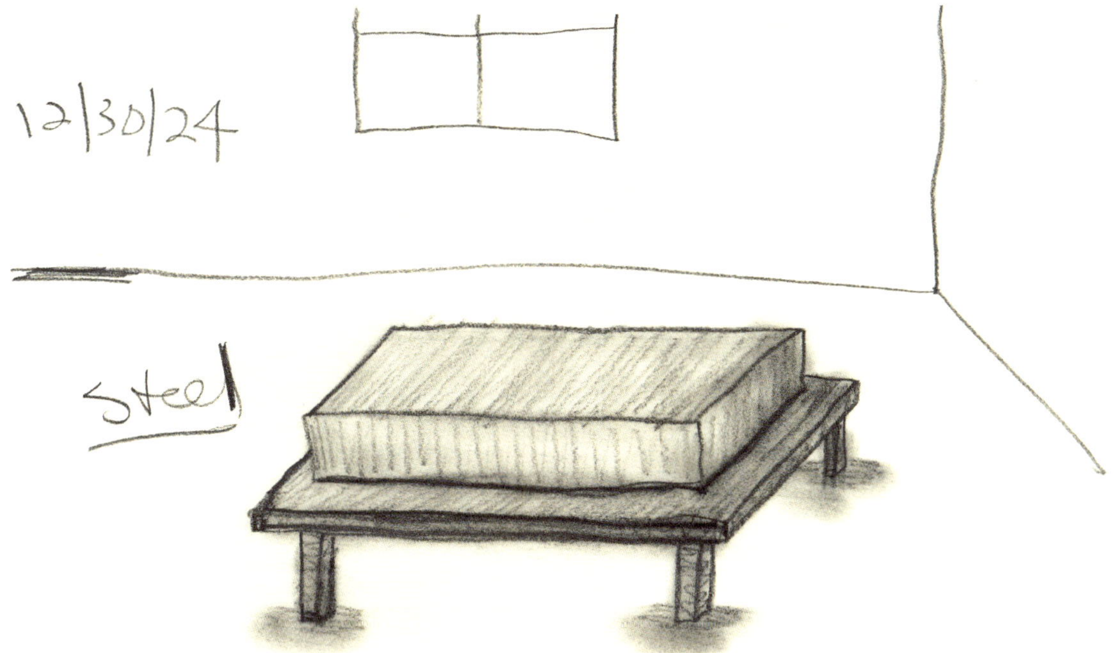

Steel

A sculpture "of":
a sculpture on a table,

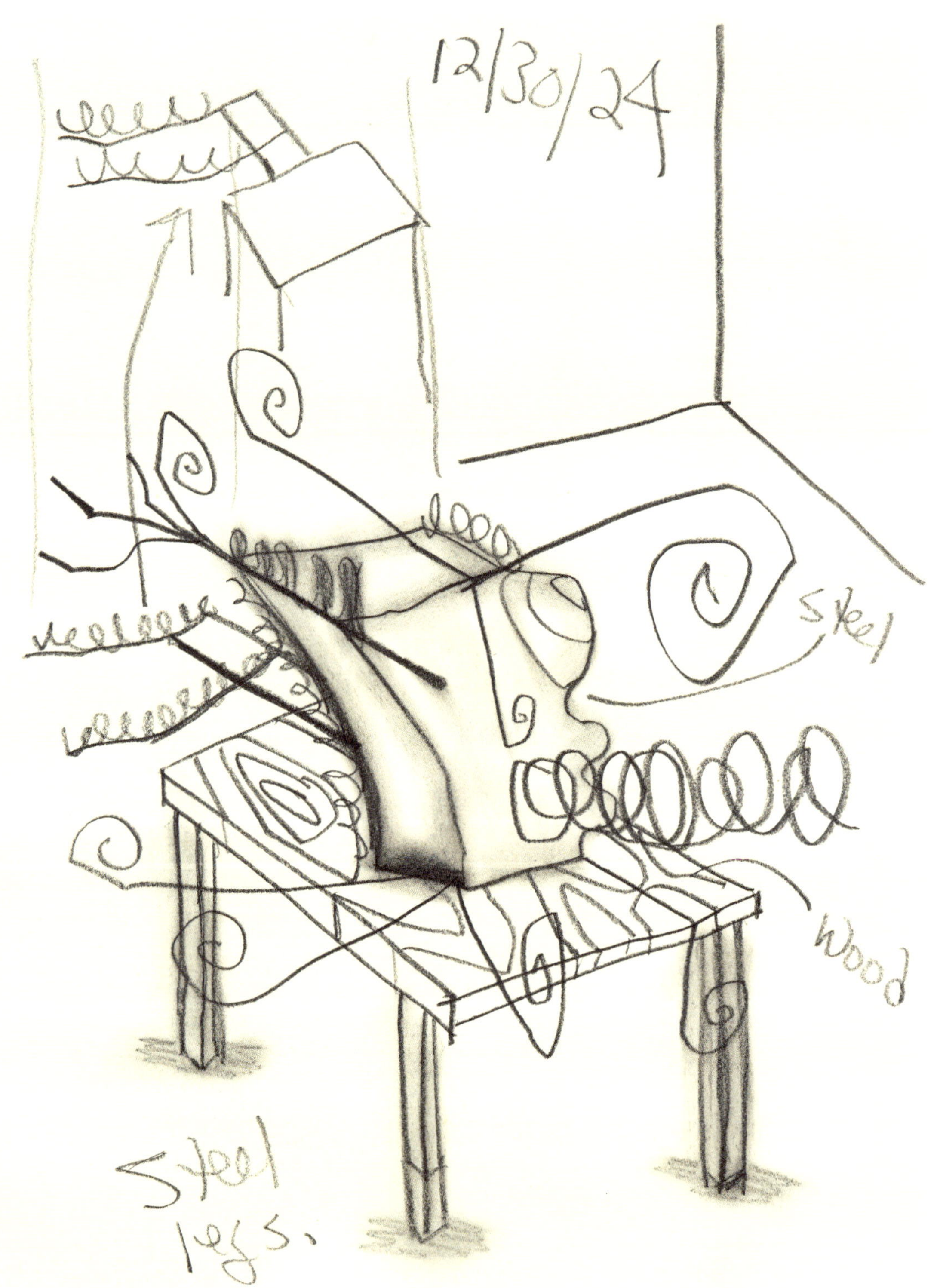

12/30/24
steel
wood
steel
legs.

Drawing Sculpture

Throughout 2022, my work gradually became focused on the subject of a sculptor who, disappointed by the opportunities presented to him within contemporary culture, gambles his future on emigrating to another world, a colony of Earth. There he builds a studio on the frontier to live and make his work among the purple humanoids who are the planet's indigenous inhabitants. As I explored the terms of this futuristic fable in my drawings and paintings, certain structural elements emerged.

The long-haired, white-skinned, bearded artist appears in or around an open orthogonal construction (the studio) set atop a curved horizon that might be a hill or the edge of the planet itself. As he attends to his work, shirtless and barefoot in baggy trousers, he is visited by the indigenous purple people. The landscape surrounding the studio is littered with boxy garbage, the uninterpretable artifacts of this distant world.

It's this last detail that is relevant to this book. I had already been doodling these open-frame cubic boxes in notebooks. Saggy and distorted, with spiraling linear extensions at their corners and frilly undulating borders along some of their edges, they were simple and mindless to draw, both repetitive and individually specific, like different members of the same species. I began deploying these things as a feature of the landscape of the larger compositions. They enriched the field with visual events, and their crude perspectival nature helped define the topography of the hillside. I wasn't sure what they represented—maybe an element of the native ecosystem of this planet, capable of self-replication but, like viruses, not obviously life. Or they might have been discarded local tech, built from both mechanical and organic components. Their lack of dispositive reference was a large part of their appeal; they were "abstract."

At some point it occurred to me that they might be sculptural refuse, either studio garbage or perhaps evidence of some art-analogous activity among the lavender locals, and that I should explore them in drawings approached from this point of view. Somewhere between the impulse and the action, I realized that I would be making drawings of sculptures—or more accurately, fantasies of sculpture—sitting on tables in crude interior spaces. I had started working on the first series of paintings of my new subject, and whenever I became antsy or indecisive in my painting studio I would go into another room and make a drawing of a sculpture. In this way the drawings in this book began to multiply.

They were strangely pleasing to make, far less fraught with emotional baggage and resistance than my paintings seem to be. I don't have a good explanation for this. I've had an aspirational yet attenuated relationship to sculpture for quite some time, and I was slightly baffled by the fact that the ostensible subject of my paintings was the making of sculpture. But the sculptures of my imaginary artist were things I would never let myself make, somewhat generic biomorphic blobs from a cartoon about modern art, sitting on the sort of bases one sees in an art school sculpture studio. I guess I would call it "bad sculpture."

An entirely different vocabulary was taking shape in the drawings. The boxy frames and spirals were getting elaborated by recursive lines, repeating loops, closed and folded planes, creating quasi-schematics of only theoretically buildable things. It occurred to me that, if realized, these would be artworks fabricated of sheet metal and metal rods, materials to which I had never given much previous thought, and their tables would have to be of very specific design to support these hypothetical objects with odd personalities. These thoughts gained force in the free space of fantasy.

It wasn't inevitable that I would try to make actual sculpture based on the drawings. I was becoming immersed in the development of the paintings, which was intermittently stressing me out, and the drawings here were a needed escape that seemed sufficient in itself—until apparently it wasn't. I decided to find a collaborator who understood the "vibe" of the drawings and who had the technical knowledge and sensitivity to help me realize their physical corollaries, and as he and I began working together I drifted away from those regular drawing interludes.

When ideas about unmade art meet actual materials and procedures, one gains a new perspective on what one is doing. As the real sculptures came into existence, I saw possibilities that were quite different from those implied by my previous drawing sessions, and I went back to drawing with those recent results in mind. This second group of drawings came about at the end of 2024 and went on for a little over a month. As drawings of sculptural possibilities, they have greater specificity than the earlier group and are more concerned with feasibility. In a way, they are "feasibility studies," which is probably both a feature and a bug. I ran out of gas with them relatively quickly, realizing that my imagination was being more vividly activated by watching my collaborators manipulate metal or by discussing the possibilities of the technology with them.

I made drawings before I considered myself an artist, and I have known since I began doing my work that drawing was the foundation of the entire activity. It has been both an end in itself and a vehicle for thinking about my paintings. A sampling of my drawings across time would be a chart of my artistic evolution, and the ones gathered here are part of that but also somewhat separated by the nature of drawing sculpture. This is partly because they represent imaginary objects, but one could say the same about studies for paintings that are never made. The difference is in the cartographic relationship between drawing and the subject of thought; when a drawing imagines a painting, both are flat rectangles, topologically equivalent, and can be mapped onto one another point for point. A drawing can be a very exact diagram or projection of the relationships on the surface of a painting that one is trying to analyze and understand. With sculpture, whether imaginary or real, no such isomorphism is possible. A drawing can imagine a complex object, but every part of the drawing can't be connected to the thing it depicts. It's not a plan. Drawing can "picture" sculpture that can't even be made, and conversely there are plenty of sculptures that can't really be drawn. Whether understood as activities or as types of things, there's an abyss between the two that can never be crossed. It's here that imagination can operate freely, and drawing is a tool to facilitate that. Fantasy comes easily and unsolicited, and so did these drawings.

Carroll Dunham
June–July 2025

Image Captions

3   *Untitled Sculpture Drawing* (12/2/23), 2023
    Pencil on paper
    8½ x 11 inches

4   *Untitled Sculpture Drawing* (12/2/23), 2023
    Watercolor marker and pencil on paper
    8½ x 11 inches

5   *Untitled Sculpture Drawing* (12/5/23), 2023
    Watercolor marker and pencil on paper
    8½ x 11 inches

6   *Untitled Sculpture Drawing* (12/16/23), 2023
    Watercolor marker and pencil on paper
    8½ x 11 inches

7   *Untitled Sculpture Drawing* (12/16/23), 2023
    Watercolor marker and pencil on paper
    8½ x 11 inches

8   *Untitled Sculpture Drawing* (12/16/23), 2023
    Watercolor marker and pencil
    8½ x 11 inches

9   *Untitled Sculpture Drawing* (12/21/23), 2023
    Watercolor marker and pencil on paper
    8½ x 11 inches

10 *Untitled Sculpture Drawing* (12/22/23), 2023
    Watercolor pencil and pencil on paper
    8½ x 11 inches

11 *Untitled Sculpture Drawing* (12/22/23), 2023
    Watercolor marker and pencil on paper
    8½ x 11 inches

12 *Untitled Sculpture Drawing* (12/23/23), 2023
    Conté crayon and pencil on paper
    8½ x 11 inches

13 *Untitled Sculpture Drawing* (12/23/23), 2023
    Conté crayon and pencil on paper
    8½ x 11 inches

14 *Untitled Sculpture Drawing* (12/24/23), 2023
    Conté crayon, watercolor marker, and pencil on paper
    8½ x 11 inches

15 *Untitled Sculpture Drawing* (12/26/23), 2023
    Conté crayon, watercolor marker, and pencil on paper
    11 x 8½ inches

16 *Untitled Sculpture Drawing* (12/29/23), 2023
    Conté crayon, watercolor marker, and pencil on paper
    11 x 8½ inches

17 *Untitled Sculpture Drawing* (12/29/23), 2023
    Conté crayon, watercolor marker, and pencil on paper
    11 x 8½ inches

18 *Untitled Sculpture Drawing* (1/27/24), 2024
    Conté crayon, watercolor marker, and pencil on paper
    11 x 8½ inches

19 *Untitled Sculpture Drawing* (1/29/24), 2024
    Conté crayon, watercolor marker, and pencil on paper
    8½ x 11 inches

20 *Untitled Sculpture Drawing* (1/29/24), 2024
    Conté crayon, watercolor marker, and pencil on paper
    8½ x 11 inches

21 *Untitled Sculpture Drawing* (1/30/24), 2024
    Conté crayon, watercolor marker, and pencil on paper
    11 x 8½ inches

22 *Untitled Sculpture Drawing* (2/13/24), 2024
    Conté crayon and watercolor marker on paper
    8½ x 11 inches

23 *Untitled Sculpture Drawing* (2/24/24), 2024
    Conté crayon, watercolor marker, and pencil on paper
    8½ x 11 inches

24 *Untitled Sculpture Drawing* (3/3/24), 2024
    Conté crayon, watercolor marker, and pencil on paper
    11 x 8½ inches

25 *Untitled Sculpture Drawing* (4/14/24), 2024
    Conté crayon, watercolor marker, and pencil on paper
    11½ x 16½ inches

26 *Untitled Sculpture Drawing* (4/14/24), 2024
    Conté crayon, watercolor marker, and pencil on paper
    11 x 8½ inches

27 *Untitled Sculpture Drawing* (4/15/24), 2024
    Conté crayon, watercolor marker, and pencil on paper
    16½ x 11½ inches

28 *Untitled Sculpture Drawing* (4/16/24), 2024
    Conté crayon, watercolor marker, and pencil on paper
    11½ x 16½ inches

29 *Untitled Sculpture Drawing* (4/16/24), 2024
    Conté crayon, watercolor marker, and pencil on paper
    16¾ x 11½ inches

30 *Untitled Sculpture Drawing* (4/17/24), 2024
    Conté crayon, watercolor marker, and pencil on paper
    16½ x 11½ inches

31 *Untitled Sculpture Drawing* (4/19/24), 2024
Conté crayon, watercolor marker, and pencil on paper
11½ x 16½ inches

32 *Untitled Sculpture Drawing* (4/23/24), 2024
Watercolor marker on paper
11 x 8½ inches

33 *Untitled Sculpture Drawing* (4/23/24), 2024
Conté crayon, watercolor marker, and pencil on paper
16½ x 11½ inches

34 *Untitled Sculpture Drawing* (4/27/24), 2024
Conté crayon, watercolor marker, and pencil on paper
11 x 8½ inches

35 *Untitled Sculpture Drawing* (5/3/24), 2024
Conté crayon, watercolor marker, and pencil on paper
11 x 8½ inches

36 *Untitled Sculpture Drawing* (5/18/24), 2024
Watercolor marker and pencil on paper
11 x 8½ inches

37 *Untitled Sculpture Drawing* (5/31/24), 2024
Conté crayon, watercolor marker, and pencil on paper
16¾ x 11½ inches

38 *Untitled Sculpture Drawing* (7/4/24), 2024
Pencil on paper
8½ x 11 inches

39 *Untitled Sculpture Drawing* (7/29/24), 2024
Pencil on paper
8½ x 11 inches

40 *Untitled Sculpture Drawing* (8/2/24), 2024
Pencil on paper
8½ x 11 inches

41 *Untitled Sculpture Drawing* (8/2/24, 8/3/24), 2024
Ballpoint pen on paper
11 x 8½ inches

42 *Untitled Sculpture Drawing* (8/3/24), 2024
Pencil on paper
8½ x 11 inches

43 *Untitled Sculpture Drawing* (8/3/24), 2024
Ballpoint pen on paper
11 x 8½ inches

44 *Untitled Sculpture Drawing* (8/3/24), 2024
Pencil on paper
8½ x 11 inches

45 *Untitled Sculpture Drawing* (8/5/24), 2024
Ballpoint pen on paper
11 x 8½ inches

46 *Untitled Sculpture Drawing* (8/6/24), 2024
Ballpoint pen on paper
11 x 8½ inches

47 *Untitled Sculpture Drawing* (8/8/24), 2024
Pencil on paper
11 x 8½ inches

48 *Untitled Sculpture Drawing* (8/12/24), 2024
Pencil on paper
11 x 8½ inches

49 *Untitled Sculpture Drawing* (8/13/24), 2024
Pencil on paper
11 x 8½ inches

50 *Untitled Sculpture Drawing* (8/14/24), 2024
Pencil on paper
8½ x 11 inches

51 *Untitled Sculpture Drawing* (8/19/24), 2024
Pencil on paper
8½ x 11 inches

52 *Untitled Sculpture Drawing* (8/21/24), 2024
Ballpoint pen and pencil on paper
11 x 8½ inches

53 *Untitled Sculpture Drawing* (8/22/24), 2024
Ballpoint pen on paper and pencil on paper
11 x 8½ inches

54 *Untitled Sculpture Drawing* (8/24/24), 2024
Watercolor marker and pencil on paper
8½ x 11 inches

55 *Untitled Sculpture Drawing* (8/25/24), 2024
Watercolor marker and pencil on paper
8½ x 11 inches

56 *Untitled Sculpture Drawing* (8/25/24), 2024
Watercolor marker and pencil on paper
11 x 8½ inches

57 *Untitled Sculpture Drawing* (9/8/24), 2024
Watercolor marker and pencil on paper
8½ x 11 inches

58 *Untitled Sculpture Drawing* (9/12/24), 2024
Watercolor marker and pencil on paper
8½ x 11 inches

59 *Untitled Sculpture Drawing* (9/14/24), 2024
Watercolor marker and pencil on paper
11 x 8½ inches

60 *Untitled Sculpture Drawing* (12/11/24), 2024
Pencil on paper
8½ x 11 inches

61 *Untitled Sculpture Drawing* (12/11/24), 2024
Pencil on paper
8½ x 11 inches

62 *Untitled Sculpture Drawing* (12/13/24), 2024
Pencil on paper
8½ x 11 inches

63   *Untitled Sculpture Drawing* (12/13/24), 2024
Pencil on paper
8½ x 11 inches

64   *Untitled Sculpture Drawing* (12/14/24), 2024
Pencil on paper
11 x 8½ inches

65   *Untitled Sculpture Drawing* (12/14/24), 2024
Pencil on paper
11 x 8½ inches

66   *Untitled Sculpture Drawing* (12/15/24), 2024
Pencil on paper
11 x 8½ inches

67   *Untitled Sculpture Drawing* (12/16/24), 2024
Pencil on paper
11 x 8½ inches

68   *Untitled Sculpture Drawing* (12/17/24), 2004
Pencil on paper
11 x 8½ inches

69   *Untitled Sculpture Drawing* (12/17/24), 2024
Pencil on paper
11 x 8½ inches

70   *Untitled Sculpture Drawing* (12/17/24), 2024
Pencil on paper
8½ x 11 inches

71   *Untitled Sculpture Drawing* (12/22/24), 2024
Pencil on paper
11 x 8½ inches

72   *Untitled Sculpture Drawing* (12/23/24), 2024
Pencil on paper
8½ x 11 inches

73   *Untitled Sculpture Drawing* (12/23/24), 2024
Pencil on paper
8½ x 11 inches

74   *Untitled Sculpture Drawing* (12/24/24), 2024
Pencil on paper
11 x 8½ inches

75   *Untitled Sculpture Drawing* (12/28/24), 2024
Pencil on paper
8½ x 11 inches

76   *Untitled Sculpture Drawing* (12/28/24), 2024
Pencil on paper
11 x 8½ inches

77   *Untitled Sculpture Drawing* (12/28/24), 2024
Pencil on paper
11 x 8½ inches

78   *Untitled Sculpture Drawing* (12/28/24), 2024
Pencil on paper
11 x 8½ inches

79   *Untitled Sculpture Drawing* (12/29/24), 2024
Pencil on paper
11 x 8½ inches

80   *Untitled Sculpture Drawing* (12/30/24), 2024
Pencil on paper
8½ x 11 inches

81   *Untitled Sculpture Drawing* (12/30/24), 2024
Pencil on paper
8½ x 11 inches

82   *Untitled Sculpture Drawing* (12/30/24), 2024
Pencil on paper
11 x 8½ inches